2759   5

D0055200

The Eucharist
in the New Testament

Zacchaeus Studies: New Testament

General Editor: Mary Ann Getty

The Eucharist
in the New Testament

by

Jerome Kodell, OSB

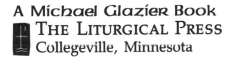

A Michael Glazier Book
THE LITURGICAL PRESS
Collegeville, Minnesota

APR 1 9 '00

BV
823
.K63
1991

AARON MEMORIAL LIBRARY
ST. MARY'S COLLEGE
ORCHARD LAKE, MICH. 48324

A Michael Glazier Book published by The Liturgical Press

Cover design by David Manahan, O.S.B.

Copyright © 1988 by Michael Glazier, Inc. Copyright © 1991 by The Order of St. Benedict, Inc., Collegeville, Minnesota. All rights reserved. No part of this book may be reproduced in any form or by any means, electronic or mechanical, including photocopying, recording, taping, or any retrieval system, without the written permission of The Liturgical Press, Collegeville, Minnesota 56321. Printed in the United States of America.

	5	6	7	8	9

Library of Congress Cataloging-in-Publication Data

Kodell, Jerome.
    The Eucharist in the New Testament / by Jerome Kodell.
       p.   cm.
    Reprint. Originally published: Wilmington, Del. : M. Glazier, 1988. (Zacchaeus studies. New Testament)
    "A Michael Glazier book."
    Includes bibliographical references and index.
    ISBN 0-8146-5663-3
    1. Lord's Supper—Biblical teaching. 2. Last Supper. 3. Bible. N.T.—Theology. I. Title. II. Series: Zacchaeus studies. New Testament.
BV823.K63   1991
234'.163'09015—dc20
                                          91-3382
                                          CIP

Dedicated to my mother,
who first taught me about the Eucharist,
and to the memory of my father,
who lived Eucharist with her and with all of us.

TABLE OF CONTENTS

Editor's Note

Zacchaeus Studies provide concise, readable and relatively inexpensive scholarly studies on particular aspects of scripture and theology. The New Testament section of the series presents studies dealing with focal or debated questions; and the volumes focus on specific texts of particular themes of current interest in biblical interpretation. Specialists have their professional journals and other forums where they discuss matters of mutual concern, exchange ideas and further contemporary trends of research; and some of their work on contemporary biblical research is now made accessible for students and others in *Zacchaeus Studies.*

The authors in this series share their own scholarship in non-technical language, in the areas of their expertise and interest. These writers stand with the best in current biblical scholarship in the English-speaking world. Since most of them are teachers, they are accustomed to presenting difficult material in comprehensible form without compromising a high level of critical judgment and analysis.

The works of this series are ecumenical in content and purpose and cross credal boundaries. They are designed to augment formal and informal biblical study and discussion. Hopefully they will also serve as texts to enhance and supplement seminary, university and college classes. The series will also aid Bible study groups, adult education and parish religious education classes to develop intelligent, versatile and challenging programs for those they serve.

Mary Ann Getty
New Testament Editor

1

Introduction

The Eucharist has been the distinctive Christian rite of worship from the earliest days of the Church. Since the Reformation, it is no longer accurate to say that the Eucharist is the central act of worship for all Christians, though it still is so for most. Churches which celebrate the Eucharist regularly look to it as a principal source of insight into the meaning of their faith and the means for renewing their bond with one another in Christ while being nourished for the spiritual journey.

The title "Eucharist" (thanksgiving) for this rite is not used in the New Testament,[1] though the verb form, "to give thanks," has a firm place in the accounts of the institution (Mk 14:23; Mt 26:27; Lk 22:17, 19; 1 Cor 11:24). St. Paul is the source of three biblical titles: "Holy Communion," derived from the translation of koinōnia in 1 Corinthians 10:16 "Table of the Lord" (1 Cor 10:31) and what may be the technical term in his communities, "the Lord's Supper" (1 Cor 11:30). Another early title, recorded by Luke, is "the Breaking of the Bread" (Lk 24:35; Acts 2:42).

There are many different approaches to the Eucharist among Christians. It has no place at all in the worship of some

---

[1] It does appear as a variant for *eulogia* (blessing) in 1 Cor 10:16 in a few Greek manuscripts of the ninth century and later. "Eucharist" was used as a title for the Lord's Supper in New Testament times, however, as we know from the Didache (IX:I) at the end of the first century. Soon after that it is found in the writings of Ignatius of Antioch (110) and Justin Martyr (150).

Christians, others celebrate it rarely; while some Churches have the Eucharist every Sunday, frequently during the week, or even daily. Among these Christian communities there is also variety in the meaning of the eucharistic ritual. The Eucharist is a commemoration or re-enactment of the Last Supper, in which the risen Lord Jesus is present symbolically or really. The bread and wine are given a different meaning or they become really different, the body and blood of the Lord. The ritual is a community meal only or it is also a sacrificial banquet.

Every Christian group looks to the New Testament as a source of its doctrine, its worship, its way of life. The diversity in eucharistic practice and understanding makes it evident that there are many ways of reading the New Testament data. It also shows that Church tradition has a powerful influence in the shaping of a Christian's attitude toward even the central realities of the faith.

This short study of the Eucharist in the New Testament will be divided into two parts. The first part seeks to uncover the origins of the Eucharist and to trace developments in the earliest eucharistic practice and understanding. The purpose will be, to use the terminology of the Biblical Commission's *Instruction on the Historical Truth of the Gospels,*[2] to determine what we can learn from the first two of the three "stages of tradition." Stage I refers to the time of the historical Jesus, Stage II to the time during which the primitive communities reflected on the life and teaching of Jesus and began to make it the focus of their worship and preaching. The purpose will be to discern what Jesus' intentions were as they are revealed in his recorded words and deeds, particularly at the Last Supper; and how the early believers understood and performed the Eucharist.

The second part of the book will investigate the eucharistic theology of the individual New Testament writers. This part of the study will focus on Stage III of the tradition, the contribution of individual believers who each brought to their

[2]April 21, 1964. See the text and commentary in Joseph A. Fitzmyer, "The Biblical Commission's Instruction on the Historical Truth of the Gospels," *TS* 25 (1964) 386-408.

presentation of the Eucharist the understanding current in their local community and their own personal insight.

This study has carefully placed boundaries. It does not presume to be a complete treatment of the Eucharist in the New Testament. The focus is on the Gospels and the teaching of Paul, the sources with the greatest influence on Church tradition.[3] The Acts of the Apostles is brought into the investigation because of its unity with the Gospel of Luke. The only writing of Paul with direct bearing on the subject is his First Letter to the Corinthians. So the study encompasses six New Testament books: the Gospels of Matthew, Mark, Luke, and John, the Acts of the Apostles, and First Corinthians.[4] All of them bear witness to the eucharistic practice and understanding of their own time, but also, in varying degrees, to the practice of earlier times and to the institution by Jesus. They permit us to trace developments as the Christian disciples quickly accepted the Last Supper as the model for their worship and probed the meaning of their sacred meal in the light of their faith in Jesus.

[3]The only other New Testament writing with substantial influence is the Letter to the Hebrews.

[4]For purposes of comparison among the Synoptic Gospels, our study presumes the priority of Mark.

Part One:

Origins

1

The Last Supper: A Starting Point

The inspiration for all the Christian eucharistic rituals is the farewell supper Jesus shared with his disciples on the night before he died. As the biblical writers describe it, Jesus treated this meal with extreme importance. He took pains to prepare for it, gave important final instructions, and invested certain gestures with great meaning. A mandate was given: "Do this in remembrance of me."

This meal, however unique, was not an isolated event in the life of Jesus. His ministry was characterized by the special role he gave to table-fellowship. He was a guest at meals with the well-to-do and respected (Mk 14:3) and with the scorned (Mk 2:15-17). He participated in wedding feasts (Jn 2:1-11), and shared meals with his friends and disciples (Lk 10:38-42). Jesus's eating habits became a byword: "Behold, a glutton and a drunkard, a friend of tax collectors and sinners!" (Mt 11:19). His open table-fellowship with all, saint or sinner, was a way of proclaiming God's forgiveness to everyone. This was very offensive to those with a more restricted idea of God and of salvation. To share a meal with someone was a particular form of intimacy that had to be protected. It meant not only sharing of food but of life. In giving himself to all, Jesus was expressing God's openness and his own vulnerable servant-hood. Later, when Judas betrayed Jesus, this was interpreted as a breach of the special covenant formed by their meals together: "He who ate my bread has lifted his heel against me" (Jn 13:18 = Ps 41:9).[1]

---

[1]Robert Karris has shown that this theme of table fellowship with the outcasts is central to the presentation of Jesus' ministry in Luke's Gospel: *Luke: Artist and*

The Last Supper of Jesus with his disciples expressed this intimacy, openness, and service in a dramatic way. The Gospels of Luke and John emphasize the theme of service, Luke by transferring the dispute about greatness to the Supper from earlier in the ministry (Lk 22:24-27; Mt 20:24-28, Mk 10:41-45), John by his footwashing scene (Jn 13:13-17). Finally, of course, service and openness and intimacy are climaxed in the sharing of the bread and wine as Jesus' body and blood.

Jesus often used meal imagery in his teaching, a favorite theme being that of the heavenly wedding banquet. This stress lent an eschatological significance to his own meals.[2] Jesus spoke of his presence among his disciples as a wedding banquet (Mk 2:19), and told the crowds that open table-fellowship now will be rewarded in the resurrection of the just (Lk 14:13-14). Those who imitate Jesus' example of service at table will eat and drink with him in the kingdom (Lk 22:30). The eschatological emphasis is brought into the Last Supper in Jesus' promise not to eat or drink until the kingdom of God comes (Mk 14:25, Lk 22:15-18).[3]

The feeding of the multitudes is also a part of the preparation for the Last Supper and the celebration of the latter Church. Mark records two stories of the miraculous multiplication of bread and fish, portraying Jesus as the one who feeds all, both Jew (Mk 6:34-43) and Gentile (8:1-9). All were satisfied and there was still food left over, symbolizing the fullness and plenty of the messianic kingdom inaugurated by Jesus. In telling these stories, the evangelists draw the connections with the Last Supper: "He blessed, broke, gave to the disciples" (Mk 6:41); "Having given thanks (*eucharistēsas*) he broke them and gave them to his disciples..." (Mk 8:6).

Theologian: Luke's Passion Account as Literature (Theological Inquiries; New York: Paulist, 1985) 47-48. See the discussion in Chapter Eight below.

[2]This is summarized succinctly in J.D.G. Dunn, *Unity and Diversity in the New Testament: An Inquiry into the Character of Earliest Christianity* (Philadelphia: Westminster, 1977) 162-63.

[3]Paul highlights this aspect in his own way, by interpreting the Lord's Supper as the proclamation of the death of the Lord "until he comes" (1 Cor 11:26).

The Supper Accounts

It is surprising to find that on a matter treated so reverently and carefully as the Last Supper, the pattern of a privileged ceremonial among Christians, there are so many discrepancies among the accounts and so many uncertainties about exactly what happened at the Supper and what it meant.

Four accounts of the Supper (the three Synoptic Gospels and 1 Corinthians) describe the institution of the Eucharist. The Gospel of John says nothing about the institution at the Supper, but he describes a foot-washing nowhere else recorded, and incorporates a lengthy discourse not found in the Synoptics. There is eucharistic teaching, however, in John 6:35-58 (especially vv 51-58), the discourse on the bread of life. The four accounts of the institution are separated into two groups or types, Mark/ Matthew and Paul/ Luke, according to their agreements or differences with one another. Mark/ Matthew, for example, contain an instruction of Jesus to "Take (and eat)" which is not in Paul/ Luke. Paul/ Luke say that the cup was shared "after the supper." They record Jesus' words over the cup as "the new covenant in my blood," while Mark/ Matthew have "This is my blood of the covenant." Remarkably, Mark/ Matthew do not have the mandate to repeat what Jesus had done, "Do this in remembrance of me," which is found in Paul and Luke. Did the tradition of Mark/ Matthew drop this mandate, or did the other tradition add it to the Supper narrative? The answer to such questions has many implications.

All the accounts place the Supper on the night before Jesus died. But there is a major discrepancy about the date of the Supper. For the Synoptics the Supper is a Passover meal, taking place on the first evening of Passover, while the lambs are being slaughtered in the temple. In John's account, the death of Jesus takes place at the hour of the sacrifice of the Passover lambs, and the Supper is held the previous night, a day earlier than in the Synoptics. Though Jesus' death is related to the Passover in John, the Last Supper is not a Passover meal.[4]

[4]Paul is noncommittal on the dating of the Supper except to say that it took place "on the night he was betrayed" (1 Cor 11:23).

All four institution narratives speak of "covenant" in connection with the cup. The reference in the version of Mark/Matthew is primarily to the Sinai covenant. After splashing half the blood from the peace offerings on the altar (representing God), Moses read the "book of the covenant" to the people, who professed adherence to it. Then he sprinkled the rest of the blood on the people, saying "This is the blood of the covenant" (Ex 24:5-8). The accounts in Paul/Luke speak of a "*new* covenant in my blood," connecting Jesus' action with the new covenant promised by Jeremiah (Jer 31:31-34). The idea of a "new" covenant is also present in the words "my blood" in the Mark/Matthew version, but the notion of the fulfillment of the Sinai covenant is stronger.

The difference here in the interpretative words over the cup is typical of the obstacles encountered when one tries to get back exactly to what Jesus did *(ipsissima facta)* and said *(ipsissima verba)* at the Last Supper. Was there one cup as in three accounts or two as in Luke? Did the apostles drink before the words of institution as in Mark (14:23-24) or afterward? Did Jesus say his blood was being poured out "for many" (Matthew/Mark) or "for you" (Luke)? The only actions and words identical in the four institution accounts are: Jesus took bread, broke it, and said: "This is my body";[5] took a cup and interpreted the meaning of it (but what he said varies, as noted above). All record also an eschatological implication of the Supper, the Synoptics in terms of the fulfillment of the kingdom, Paul in terms of the coming back of the risen Lord.

Why have these discrepancies in the reports of the Last Supper been tolerated to remain? Why has not some editor brought them into agreement with one another? The first memories of what Jesus had said and done at the Supper passed by word of mouth among the early disciples. The details varied in the telling, and different communities developed distinctive narratives. The conviction that Jesus was soon to return in glory apparently neutralized any urge to keep careful records for subsequent generations. It was twenty years

---

[5]The Greek of this phrase is identical in the accounts *(touto estin to sōma mou)*—except that in 1 Corinthians *mou* is after *touto*—which is strong evidence that very early this was the accepted rendition of the Hebrew or Aramaic expression.

after the death and resurrection of Jesus that our first New Testament document appeared (1 Thessalonians), and most of the Christian Scriptures were written fifty and more years after that epochal event. By the time our narratives were gathered together, probably no one knew what the exact course of events or the precise wording of Jesus' statements at the Supper had been. This was not important, as long as the narratives substantially agreed in their reports.

Another reason the narratives were not edited into conformity was the respect for "tradition," what had been handed down from the earliest times. All of the accounts we possess have been affected by liturgical usage. The outline of the Last Supper and the words and actions of Jesus were simplified and stylized for use in the Lord's Supper. Once the tradition of the Last Supper entered liturgical practice, its holding power became greater than ever. Thus when we study the biblical narratives of the Supper, we find not just reports of a historical event, but the Church's developing understanding of the significance of the Supper as it deepened under the post-resurrection guidance of the Holy Spirit.

Without going into detail or dealing with discrepancies among the accounts, we may give the following as a general outline of what the writers describe as happening at the Last Supper. At a festive meal on the eve of his death, which may have been a Passover meal, Jesus gave a new interpretation to a familiar Jewish family/social ritual. During the main course of the meal, acting as the host or as the *paterfamilias* he said a blessing over the bread, broke it, and passed it to his friends, saying, "This is my body." After the main meal, he held a cup of wine (the third or fourth in a Paschal meal), blessed it as he had the bread, and gave it to the rest with words identifying the wine as his blood. The disciples understood that Jesus was sharing himself with them in an intimate way through this gesture. The convictions which appear in the Supper narratives include the understanding that Jesus is foretelling his death, a death which will bring forgiveness of sins: that he is inaugurating a new covenant, that this meal is a harbinger of the banquet in the kingdom, and that he is giving them something to imitate.

2

The Last Supper
and the Lord's Supper:
a Survey of Recent Scholarship

The early Christian community's experience of the Eucharist has influenced the way the Last Supper is presented in the
biblical accounts. The result is that the New Testament model
for the Eucharist is really two models, converging in the
Christian liturgical tradition from two different but interacting
sources: the Last Supper and the Lord's Supper. The
distinction is between the final meal Jesus shared with his
disciples before he died and the community re-enactment of
that meal after Jesus' death and resurrection. Some unravel-
ing of the accounts is needed to trace the developments from
the Last Supper to the Lord's Supper. The difficulty is
increased by the very nature and purpose of the Last Supper
narratives, which are not complete historical descriptions, but
are limited to key elements in a stylized form. The inevitable
question is: how much of the description is projected back to
Jesus' time through the prism of Christian liturgical experience, and how much historical fact is retrievable from the Last
Supper narratives?

The question is not idle. Earlier in this century, the critical
German school drew up a strong case against the historical
basis for the Last Supper accounts. The accounts were
described as "cult etiologies," that is, they were stories created
by the evangelists or by their communities to provide a
historical basis for the practice of the Lord's Supper. A less

radical approach did allow for the historicity of the Last Supper, but maintained that the biblical accounts are completely tailored by cultic usage.[1] Though there has been a softening of this approach, it is still possible to find the extreme view expressed, as in Herbert Braun's statement: "The final meal (Mk 14:22-25) may be a reading back of the Lord's Supper as celebrated in Hellenistic Christian communities into the last days of Jesus, since the meal shows the marks of Hellenistic sacramental religion, and it is difficult to find a place for it in Palestinian or even in Qumran religious thinking."[2]

Jeremias

The major counteroffensive to this position was launched by Joachim Jeremias in his *The Eucharistic Words of Jesus,* which appeared in 1935 and has been a standard source for study of the Supper narratives ever since. Jeremias placed the four accounts of the institution, the core of the Last Supper tradition, under the microscope of his minute investigation. He found that the liturgical practice of the Christian community had indeed influenced the formulation of the Supper narratives in many ways. His evidence showed that "the eucharistic words of Jesus are available to us exclusively in the form of liturgical texts." But he went on to state what he called "the really important thing"—that discernible underneath or embedded in the liturgical tradition is "an element that cannot be derived from the worship, *a preliturgical stratum of tradition.*"[3]

Jeremias' method was to reconstruct the original Hebrew or Aramaic wording behind the Greek texts. This, he felt, would be a significant step in determining which of the two types of

[1]Rudolf Bultmann, *Theology of the New Testament* (London: SCM, 1952) I, 144-51.

[2]*Jesus* (Stuttgart, 1969) 50, quoted in I. H. Marshall, *Last Supper and Lord's Supper* (Grand Rapids: Eerdmans, 1980), 30-31.

[3]Joachim Jeremias, *The Eucharistic Words of Jesus* (New York: Scribner's, 1966) 137.

narratives, Mark/ Matthew or Paul/ Luke, had the best claim to originality. Paul's account in 1 Corinthians was, of course, the earliest of the documents. It records "what I also delivered to you" (11:23) at the time of the founding of the community at Corinth by Paul around the year 50. Paul himself had probably learned this from the community at Antioch in the mid-40's, which means that his form of the tradition goes back to about a decade after the event.

Jeremias gave due weight to the antiquity of this source, but he realized that the antiquity of a document is not the only factor in determining the antiquity of traditions: primitive traditions may be preserved in later documents. Thus he found that Luke's version of the institution, written about thirty years later, contained elements differing from Paul's which came from a pre-Pauline stage of transmission.[4] His overall conclusion was that of all the accounts, that of Mark (on which Matthew is based), dating from about 70, contains the oldest form of the primitive Semitic tradition, which goes back "into the first decade after the death of Jesus."[5]

These findings of Jeremias went against the tide of critical German scholarship when they first appeared; over the years they were subjected to vigorous review resulting in some modifications by Jeremias, but he held to his general view and won support for most of it. Some of Jeremias' views still questioned are the definition of a "Semitism," the idea that more Semitisms in a document mean greater antiquity, and the conviction that by reconstructing the original language we can get back to the *ipsissima verba Jesu,* the very words that Jesus spoke at the Last Supper. Jeremias' overall thesis, however, that there is a historical kernel in the Last Supper accounts, has not been overturned. His conviction on this point more and more governs modern research.

---

[4]The two elements isolated by Jeremias were Luke's omission of the copula *estin* (is) in 22:20 and the omission of the second remembrance-word: *Eucharistic Words,* 185, 188.

[5]*Ibid.,* 196.

Lietzmann

Meanwhile, another kind of debate was going on. In 1926, Hans Lietzmann had published *Mass and Lord's Supper,* [6] in which he argued that in the beginning there were two distinct forms of the Christian Eucharist, a Jerusalem form and a Pauline form. The Jerusalem Eucharist corresponded to the breaking of the bread mentioned in Acts 2:42-46 in which there was strong emphasis on table fellowship and on the joy of celebrating in the presence of the risen Lord. This type of the Eucharist was understood as a continuation of the meals the disciples shared with Jesus during his ministry and was completely disassociated from the Last Supper. It had no words of institution and none of the themes of sacrifice or atonement usually associated with the Eucharist. It gave great weight to the eschatological significance of the fellowship meals as anticipations of the messianic banquet of heaven.

The Pauline form of the Eucharist, which is represented for Lietzmann in Mark's account as well, concentrates on the death of Christ rather than on the joy of fellowship and eschatological anticipation and is characterized by Hellenistic sacrificial concepts. This Pauline form eventually displaced the Jerusalem form and prevailed everywhere.[7]

Lietzmann's thesis did not carry the day, but it did set off a spirited discussion among scholars. One of the principal spin-offs was the theory of Ernst Lohmeyer, writing a decade later (1937), who supported the general view but linked the two types of Eucharist to a theory of two types of Christianity, that of Galilee and that of Jerusalem. According to him, the post-resurrection meals described by Lietzmann were patterned on the meals of Jesus' Galilean ministry; while the Lord's Supper described by Paul and reflected in the Last Supper accounts of the Synoptics was actually the Eucharist current in Jerusalem.[8]

[6] *Messe und Herrenmahl;* (English: Leiden: Brill, 1953-68).

[7] A. J. B. Higgins, "H. Lietzmann's 'Mass and Lord's Supper' (Messe und Herrenmahl)," *Expository Times* 65 (1954) 335. See also the thorough discussion in R. H. Fuller, "The Double Origin of the Eucharist," *BR* 8 (1963) 60-72.

[8] Eduard Schweizer, *The Lord's Supper According to the New Testament* (Facet Book; Philadelphia: Fortress, 1967) 23.

Another theory from this discussion made the two forms of the Eucharist consequential rather than contemporary: first came the fellowship celebrations of the "breaking of the bread"; as Christianity moved into the Hellenistic world, more and more Passover and sacrifice themes were evoked. The positive result of the debate was to call attention to the various influences from Jesus' life and ministry and from the Last Supper which coalesced in the Lord's Supper as celebrated in the early Church. No doubt the eschatological theme, which had been a feature of Jesus' preaching, was clearer at the time of the Last Supper and in the first Eucharists than some of the other emphases which were developed later. But the contention that from the beginning there were two quite distinct kinds of Eucharist is untenable.[9]

Another question springing from Lietzmann's research was whether or not the Lord's Supper was sometimes celebrated without wine. In Palestinian custom of the time, wine was not drunk at ordinary meals. Supporting the idea that only bread was used at some early Eucharists were the naming of the rite as "the breaking of the bread" and the thrust of the Johannine "bread of life" discourse, which says nothing about wine (John 6:35-59). The use of the word "body" *(sōma)* instead of "flesh" *(sarx)* was also taken as an indication, since "flesh" contrasts with "blood," but "body" can be taken to mean flesh and blood. The very point about the originality of the eschatological theme defeats this theory, since the eschatological sayings of the Last Supper are always connected with the wine.[10]

Schürmann

After Jeremias, the next thoroughgoing analysis of the Supper accounts to arouse wide interest was made by Heinz Schürmann during the 1950's.[11] His research appeared in

---

[9] Higgins, "Lietzmann," 336.

[10] Schweizer, *The Lord's Supper,* 25.

[11] It is amazing that John Reumann, in his wide-ranging survey of recent research on the Supper narratives, fails to mention Schürmann: *The Supper of the Lord: The New*

several articles but was summarized in a trilogy on Luke's Supper account. The three installments were: I. The Account of the Paschal Meal; II. The Institution Account; III. Jesus' Farewell Discourse.[12]

Schürmann followed the lead of Jeremias in rejecting the pessimism of liberal scholarship about the historicity of the Last Supper or the retrievability of factual information. But he challenged Jeremias' findings in some important areas. Jeremias had presented Mark's account as based on the most primitive tradition because of its use of Semitisms. Schürmann questioned both the method of determining Semitisms and the cogency of the overall argument: even if Semitisms are present in the Greek text, this may show only that the text was handed on in a Palestinian rather than a Hellenistic community. The Greek-flavored text could have originated from an equally primitive tradition.

Schürmann, in fact, maintained that the earliest tradition of the Last Supper was contained in the Gospel of Luke, the most Hellenistic of the four Gospels. The differences between Luke and Mark (and Matthew) derived most of all from Luke's use of a written account of the Supper which is older than any of the Gospel accounts. This early narrative is behind Luke 22:15-20 (the first cup, the bread), 22:24-32 (the dispute among the apostles; the promise of judging the twelve tribes in the kingdom; the words to Peter), and 22:35-38 (the two swords). The remaining verses (7-14, 21-23, 33-34) are Luke's redactional re-working of Mk 14:12-17, 18b-21, 29-31.

Two of Schürmann's conclusions were responses to major textual debates. Many scholars considered Lk 22:15-18 a Lucan reworking of the eschatological saying in Mk 14:25. Schürmann joined Jeremias in establishing that these verses derive from a pre-Marcan tradition and are not dependent on the present text of Mark. In fact, Mk 14:25 comes from the

Testament, Ecumenical Dialogues, and Faith and Order on Eucharist (Philadelphia: Fortress, 1985) 1-52.

[12]H. Schürmann, *Eine quellenkritischen Untersuchung des lukanischen Abendmahlsberichtes Lk 22, 7-38. I. Der Paschamahlbericht Lk 22, (7-14) 15-18. II. Der Einsetzungsbericht Lk 22, 19-20. III. Jesu Abschiedsrede Lk 22, 21-38.* (Neutestamentliche Abhandlungen XIX, 5; XX, 4: XX, 5 ; Münster: Aschendorff, 1953, 1955, 1957).

same source and is the only remaining verse of the series which would have paralleled Luke's. In the question of the long or short text of Luke 22:15-20, Schürmann agreed again with Jeremias on the authenticity of the longer text, (that is, including verses 19b-20), but did not agree that the text was part of a liturgical formula. It came from the primitive written account mentioned before. Though Luke's version is close to that of Paul in 1 Corinthians, Luke did not copy Paul. Luke and Paul used independently the earlier source, a source not known to Mark.

Thus Schürmann challenged the Marcan priority espoused by Jeremias in favor of a Lucan (and Pauline) priority. But underlying this debate was a common assumption which had grown more cogent because of support from different directions: the Last Supper texts are not creations of the evangelists or of the worshipping community. They show evidence of liturgical tradition and of editorial revisions. But at the heart there is a core that goes back to the earliest Christian community and to Jesus himself.

Ongoing Discussion

Other scholars were reacting to the position of Jeremias and, as time went on, Schürmann. As Jeremias' work went into further editions over the subsequent decades, the climate became more favorable for a search into the historicity of the Last Supper. The radical German school gave way to the post-Bultmannians with their "New Quest for the Historical Jesus."[13] Out of this circle came Günther Bornkamm's *Jesus of Nazareth* which treated the Supper as historical, and sought to determine Jesus' own motive and understanding of the event.[14]

Eduard Schweizer was another proponent of the priority of Paul/Luke over Mark/Matthew and supported the findings of Schürmann on this point. However, Schweizer considered the Pauline account to be more primitive than the Lucan,

[13]See Raymond E. Brown, "After Bultmann, What?—An Introduction to the Post-Bultmannians," *CBQ* 26 (1964) 1-30.

[14](New York: Harper and Row, 1960) 160-163.

rather than vice versa. The eschatological tradition which influenced both Luke and Mark is later than that which Paul transmits.[15] The same kind of position was defended by Paul Neuenzeit in his 1960 dissertation on the Lord's Supper. 1 Corinthians 11 reflects a more primitive tradition than Mark 14. Neuenzeit agrees on the authenticity of the longer Lucan text in the Supper account, but not on the priority of Luke over Paul.[16]

The question of the paschal character of the Last Supper continued to be debated, even though Schürmann had not focused much attention on it. Neuenzeit found that the Passover is not significant for Paul's theology of the Eucharist. Bornkamm concluded against Jeremias that the meal was not paschal. The question was given a thorough airing (without a conclusion) by J. Delorme in "The Last Supper and the Pasch in the New Testament," one of the essays in a symposium which appeared originally in *Lumière et Vie* (1957) and had wide circulation in book form.[17]

In Roman Catholic reflection on the origin and meaning of the Eucharist, the 1960's are associated especially with the work of Johannes Betz. His canvas is broader than Schürmann's, encompassing developments during the patristic age as well as the data of the New Testament.[18] For Betz, the Semitic origin of phrases in the Supper accounts, and the agreement in understanding of the Supper between the two major textual traditions, make an ironclad argument for the historicity of the Last Supper. Not only that, but the meaning attributed to the action comes from Jesus himself, not from the community's reflection on that event or its experience of the Lord's Supper. The original Aramaic or Hebrew account was

[15]Schweizer, *The Lord's Supper*, 28.

[16]*Das Herrenmahl. Studien zur paulinischen Eucharistieauffassung* (Munich: Kösel, 1960).

[17]The Eucharist in the New Testament (Baltimore: Helicon, 1964) 21-67. The other contributors were P. Benoit, J. Dupont, M. E. Boismard, and D. Mollat. Their mid-50's work is in dialogue with both Jeremias and Schürmann.

[18]Betz' major work was the 2-volume study, *Die Eucharistie in der Zeit der griechischen Väter* (Freiburg: Herder, 1955, 1961. This was followed by a series of articles on the theology of the Eucharist through the 1960's and 1970's.

translated into Greek during the first decade after Jesus' death, which leaves insufficient time for the kind of community theologizing posited by some critics.

Jesus saw death coming, a death flowing from his fulfillment of the mission given him by the Father. He was convinced that the sacrifice of his life would be accepted by God and lead to a new order of salvation. The Last Supper was a farewell meal like those described for the dying patriarchs of Israel in Jewish literature. His words and actions at the Supper were a symbolic expression of the meaning of his life and death. In Betz' succinct phrasing, Jesus gave his messianic being and his work "concentrated expression in a visible and even edible blessing, and bequeathed them as a sacrament."[19]

The blessing in this case, as always in Jewish festivity and ritual, was *berakah,* an expression of praise to God for his marvelous saving deeds. The Greek word which translates this most directly is *eulogia,* found in verb form in the institution accounts (Mk 14:23; Mt 26:27). This was sometimes paralleled by *eucharistein* (giving thanks: Lk 22:19; 1 Cor 11:24; see Mk 14:23; Mt 26:27). *Eucharistia* eventually became the preferred technical term for the Christian reenactment, but the meaning of *berakah* is still the key to its interpretation.[20] Going beyond the question of the paschal character of the Last Supper, Betz notes that, whoever is correct in the chronology of the events, the Synoptics or John, the New Testament nowhere interprets the Eucharist in the light of the Passover.[21]

Schürmann's premise of the priority of the Lucan tradition of the Last Supper continued (and continues) to be debated. S. Dockx argued for the originality of Mark, finding the primitive narrative in 14:17a, 18a, 23, 24a, 25. This would mean that the words of institution were added later and that the meaning of Jesus' words and actions was solely eschatological.[22] This line of thought has not appealed to others.

---

[19]"Eucharist I. Theological," *Sacramentum Mundi* (New York: Herder and Herder, 1968), Vol. 2, 258.

[20]See Thomas J. Talley, "From *Berakah* to *Eucharistia:* A Reopening Question," *Worship* 50 (1976) 115-37, and the discussion in the next Chapter.

[21]Betz, "Eucharist I. Theological," 259.

[22]S. Dockx, "Le récit du repas pascal. Marc 14, 17-26," *Bib* 46 (1965) 445-53.

Though more and more a consensus has grown for the authenticity of the longer text in Luke, there have been some strong dissenting voices. Arthur Vööbus argued to the shorter text by the use of composition criticism: Lk 22:19b-20 does not appear to be in harmony with Luke's allusions to eucharistic practice elsewhere in his writing, or with the commentary in surrounding verses.[23] According to Martin Rese, Luke transformed the institution account of his Marcan source into a complete farewell meal. The cup-word order of Luke was a problem, however, and to solve it the extra verses were added.[24]

Patsch

The growing confidence of exegetes in the possibility of retrieving the purpose of Jesus and the meaning of his words and actions at the Last Supper is typified by Hermann Patsch's *Abendmahl und historischer Jesus.*[25] Patsch seeks to show how the Supper was prepared for during the ministry of Jesus. The death of Jesus came upon the disciples as a shattering blow (Lk 24:18-24), but this was not because Jesus had not tried to prepare them. Patsch puts much weight on the ransom-saying in Mk 10:45, in which Jesus alludes to Isa 53:10 to interpret his ministry. Jesus conceived of his vocation as one of vicarious suffering, like that of the Servant. The ransom-saying is echoed in the cup-saying of Mk 22:24, "blood ... poured out for many." Thus Patsch rejects the theory that the expiation theme is a later interpretation by the Church.[26]

Patsch holds with Schürmann for the independence of Lk 22:15-18 from Mk 14:25. The two are based independently on an earlier tradition. Mark has removed the Passover allusion

[23]A. Vööbus, "Kritische Beobachtungen über die lukanische Darstellung des Herrenmahls," *ZNW* 61 (1970) 102-110.

[24]M. Rese, "Zur Problematik von Kurz—und Langtext in Luk, xxii. 17ff.," *NTS* 22 (1975) 15-31.

[25]"Last Supper and Historical Jesus" (Calwer Theologische Monographien; Stuttgart: Calwer Verlag, 1972).

[26]*Ibid.,* 169.

from the eschatological saying because it was not relevant for his community, but Mark has preserved the more primitive form of the cup-saying. The *anamnēsis*-saying (Lk 22:19; 1 Cor 11:24-25) is not original. Its absence from Mark is an insuperable difficulty because sayings of Jesus tend to grow rather than diminish in the gospel tradition, and there is no plausible reason Mark would have omitted this important mandate from the lips of Jesus. Patsch judges that the Last Supper was a Passover meal even though there are no traces of the Passover theme in the institution accounts.

In the final section of his study. Patsch draws theological implications for the sharing of the immediate disciples in the Last Supper and the participation of future Christians in the Lord's Supper. By sharing the bread and cup, the disciples receive a share in Jesus' life and work. Thus the sacramental aspect is firmly grounded in the biblical texts and in the life of Jesus.[27]

The Decade 1976-86

The recent decade has seen a strong continuation of the trend toward establishing the historicity of the Last Supper accounts and looking to them with some confidence as witnesses to the intentions of Jesus. This is a far cry from the consensus of radical scholarship early in this century. Rudolf Pesch's *Das Abendmahl und Jesu Todesverständnis*[28] agrees with Jeremias, Schürmann and others that the accounts of the Last Supper take us back to the historical event.

Pesch is closer to Jeremias in affirming Marcan priority and

---

[27] *Ibid.,* 226-230. Patsch's views on these points seem to be a more accurate reflection of the trend in scholarly consensus than are the 1975 survey findings of F. Hahn, who attributes much more to later Church development: "Zur Stand der Erforschung des urchristlichen Herrenmahls," *EvT* 35 (1975) 553-563.

[28] "The Last Supper and Jesus' Understanding of his Death" (Quaestiones Disputatae 80; Freiburg: Herder, 1978). See also the treatment in his massive commentary on Mark: *Das Markusevangelium: II. Kommentar zu Kap. 8:27 - 16, 20* (Herders theologischer Kommentar zum Neuen Testament 2/2; Freiburg: Herder, 1976) 364-377.

in his optimism about getting back to Jesus' own words.[29] He maintains that the Marcan account is not colored by the early community's liturgical experience, but is a primitive narrative report of the Last Supper. Matthew, of course, is dependent on it. Part of Luke's account (22:15-18) is a redaction of Mark and another part (22:19-20) is based on traditions behind Mark and 1 Corinthians. The only candidate besides Mark for originality according to Pesch is Paul; but Pesch finds Paul's account to be cult-etiological, disconnected from the historical Last Supper and based on the post-resurrection Lord's Supper. Pesch is convinced that the Last Supper was a Passover meal, a point which is emphasized in his interpretation of its meaning.[30]

Pesch does not argue his case merely to establish Marcan priority. His main purpose is to show that this text takes us back not only to the figure of the historical Jesus at the Last Supper, but to Jesus' own understanding of what the Supper meant. The Bultmannians doubted that the biblical accounts take us any further back than the cultic experience of the early Church. A middle position holds that the reports' historical core comes from the event, but that the interpretations cannot be attributed with certainty to Jesus. Pesch's position is that the Supper account in Mark contains the revelation of Jesus' own understanding of the meaning of his death. In Pesch's view, this means Jesus, in speaking of the "blood of the covenant shed for many," is expressing his conviction that his death (as the Isaianic Servant of God) will bring universal atonement. His death will be the crowning fulfillment of his life

---

[29]Robert Daly remarks that it is interesting that Schürmann, a Lucan authority, argues for the priority of Luke's Last Supper account, and that Pesch, a Marcan expert, favors Mark's account: "The Eucharist and Redemption: The Last Supper and Jesus' Understanding of His Death," *BTB* 11 (1981) 23.

[30]Pesch's view on this point is probably the minority opinion today. Other contemporary scholars who consider the Last Supper a Passover meal are Aulen, Bahr, Gregg, and Patsch. Among those who think it was not are Bornkamm, R. Brown, Fuller, Gese, Léon-Dufour, Schweizer, and Taylor. A few who hold for a Passover meal do so by calendar theories which harmonize the divergent Gospel chronologies: in the past, Billerbeck and Jaubert; more recently, Hoehner and Marshall. See Marshall, *Last Supper,* 71-75, and the discussion below.

and preaching and inaugurate a new covenant.[31]
I.H. Marshall notes a form-critical difference in the Supper accounts. Paul's account in 1 Corinthians is limited to the central elements of the Last Supper, but the Synoptics present these elements in the context of the story of Jesus' last night with his disciples.[32] Paul describes the part of the Supper which served as a pattern for the Lord's Supper being celebrated at a later date in Paul's communities; he tells what Jesus did in order to provide an example of what to do "in remembrance of me." The Gospels give a historical report in the context of the story of Jesus.

Which source is nearest the event of the Last Supper? Paul's is the earliest written source, but it is in a liturgical form, a sign of community reworking; but the Synoptic accounts also show liturgical influence. The Gospel accounts are edited versions of the kind of historical narratives from which developed the liturgical formula found in Paul. It seems that Marshall is leading up to a conclusion of Marcan priority, but eventually he argues for the priority of the Paul/Luke tradition.

Theories which attempt to harmonize the contradictory Holy Week chronologies of the Synoptics and John are generally in disfavor in current scholarship, but Marshall has found this line of thought persuasive again. He reports on various theories involving different Jewish calendars, including the Tuesday-evening chronology of Annie Jaubert, which aroused considerable interest in the 1950's and 1960's.[33] But he falls back on the explanation associated with the name of Paul Billerbeck, involving a dispute between the Pharisees and the Sadducees.[34]

According to this explanation, it was Jewish custom to

---

[31]Pesch is in general agreement with Patsch in this important area. See the similar conclusions of R.Schwager, "Geht die Eucharistie auf Jesus zurück?", *Orientierung* 20 (1975) 220-23. The views of Schürmann and Pesch are analyzed in John P. Galvin, "Jesus' Approach to Death: An Examination of Some Recent Studies," *TS* 41 (1980) 716-23, 723-29.

[32]*Last Supper,* 33-34.

[33]A. Jaubert, *The Date of the Last Supper* (Staten Island: Alba House, 1965). This theory will be discussed in Chapter Four.

[34]See Strack-Billerbeck, *Kommentar zum Neuen Testament aus Talmud und Midrasch* (Munich: Beck, 1928) IV/1, 41-76.

intercalate extra days at the end of certain months to keep the lunar calendar of months in line with the solar calendar of years. In order to delay the Passover one day until the Sabbath, the Sadducees added a day to the preceding month, making 15 Nisan (Passover) fall on a Saturday. The Pharisees refused to accept this change and held to 15 Nisan on Friday. Jesus followed the Pharisaic practice, which means that the Synoptic report was accurate from that point of view: the Supper took place on Thursday evening, the beginning of 15 Nisan, and the crucifixion took place on Friday afternoon. John viewed the chronology from the Sadducean point of view: the Supper took place on Thursday evening, the beginning of 14 Nisan, and the crucifixion took place on Friday afternoon, shortly before the beginning of the Passover (and the time of the Passover meal). That is why the Last Supper was understood as a Passover meal by Jesus and the Synoptic evangelists, but as a pre-Passover meal by John.

Marshall records the criticism of Jeremias that the theory's weakness is that is is "wholly conjectural." No evidence has been discovered to support the idea that Passover lambs were sacrificed in the temple on two consecutive days.[35]

In the final section of his book, Marshall reviews aspects of the meaning of the Lord's Supper in the Supper accounts and in allusions elsewhere in the New Testament. He synthesizes the various emphases into five theological themes: the Lord's Supper "stands in continuity with the acts of God in the Old Testament, brings out the saving significance of the Lord's death, is an occasion for communion with the risen Lord, is an anticipation of the heavenly banquet, and is an expression of fellowship within the body of Christ."[36]

In 1982, Xavier Léon-Dufour brought together the results

---

[35] Jeremias, *Eucharistic Words,* 23-24.

[36] Marshall, *Last Supper,* 154. Marshall, a Methodist, is a respected biblical scholar who uses modern critical methods within a conservative approach. But his confessional stance inclines him to take a radical view of the meaning of the Eucharist, so that he denies any dynamic sacramental significance to the words and actions of Jesus. Ecumenically, this seems to be a backward step from a biblically-based doctrinal convergence among Roman Catholics, Lutherans, Anglicans and some other Churches during recent years. See R. H. Fuller's review in *ATR* 64 (1982) 585-86.

of several articles in a lengthy study, *Le Partage du pain eucharistique selon le nouveau Testament.*[37] Beginning with a study of the practice of the Lord's Supper in the early Church, Léon-Dufour presents what he calls a "synchronic" description of the Supper accounts. He finds that they revolved around three "axes": Jesus and God's creation, Jesus and his relation to the disciples, and time past, present, future. In the second part, using a more familiar mode of discussion, Léon-Dufour traces the development of the texts through four main stages of community reflection.

The first stage was the concept of a community meal based on the Jewish *todah,* a thank offering involving the gift of bread and the narration of the Lord's intervention bringing deliverance from some sickness or tragedy (Lev 7:12-15).[38] The *todah* was permeated by the remembrance of the covenant and was a kind of covenant renewal; as Christian community reflection deepened, the theme of the new covenant, a second stage (through Jer 31:31-34), and the atoning covenant, a third stage (based on the Song of the Servant in Isaiah 53), gave more precise meaning to the Last Supper and to the worship based on it. Finally, the texts show emphasis on the presence of the risen Lord in the celebration.

The Supper accounts reveal two complementary traditions: the cultic and the testamentary. Jesus sacramentalized the customary breaking of bread and sharing of wine. All the writers emphasize the cultic element, but especially the Mark/Matthew tradition, which has simplified the bread/cup parallel. The testament of the departing hero, well known from late Jewish literature, stresses the role of Jesus as example or model. This is emphasized in the expanded Supper narrative of Luke, the lengthiest among the Synoptics, and through the remembrance commandment in Luke and in 1 Corinthians.

---

[37]"The Sharing of the Eucharistic Bread according to the New Testament" (Parole de Dieu; Paris: Ed. du Seuil, 1982).

[38]The *todah* has received a lot of attention recently in discussions of the origins of the Lord's Supper, particularly among liturgical scholars. Léon-Dufour mentions his debt especially to Cesare Giraudo, *La structura letteraria della Preghiera eucaristica. Saggio sulla genesi letteraria di una forma. Toda veterotestamentaria, Beraka giudaica, Anafora cristiana* (AnBib 92; Rome: Pontifical Biblical Institute, 1981). The *todah* will be discussed in the following Chapter.

Léon-Dufour does not think the Last Supper was a Passover meal, and in an appendix answers Jeremias' arguments on this question point by point.

Summary

The radical scepticism of scholars early in this century has given way to growing confidence in the historical trustworthiness of the eucharistic institution accounts. This shift is due in large part to the leadership of Joachim Jeremias in his direct challenge to critical pessimism beginning in the 1930's. But the sceptical position served the cause by forcing more thorough research and careful analysis.

Today most Catholic and Protestant critics agree in principle on the trustworthiness of the Supper accounts, and have even drawn closer on the sacramental implications.[39] Scholarly debate continues on many issues, however; for example, how much in the accounts is attributable to Jesus and how much to the Church, whether the Last Supper was a Passover meal, and how the interdependency of the traditions is to be understood.

---

[39]See, for example, the fruit of the U. S. Lutheran-Catholic dialogue: *The Eucharist as Sacrifice* (1967), *Eucharist and Ministry* (1970), *The Eucharist* (1980).

3

Jewish Meals in the First Century

When Jesus and his friends gathered in the upper room for the Last Supper, they participated in a Jewish family, social, even religious ritual which they all understood. It is clear that Jesus did something new within this established format. The accounts we possess concentrate on the unique actions and words of this Supper, streamlining or omitting the ordinary details. There was no point for the first witnesses to describe customary meal practices to other Jews. They reported on the elements which struck them as different.

This makes it difficult for later interpreters to re-create the context for the institution of the Eucharist. What kind of meal was the Last Supper, and at what part or parts of the meal did Jesus perform the actions and utter the words which gave a new meaning to the customary meal? This information is not essential for forming an understanding of the Eucharist, but knowledge of the context may uncover nuances and subtle emphases in what Jesus said and did. When reports differ about the order of events or the phrasing of the sayings, data about the ordinary ritual of the meal may help in establishing the original pattern.

Daily Jewish Meals

The Jews of Jesus' time were part of a world which reverenced the formal meal as an important family and social ritual. This was true with varying emphases in the larger

Greco-Roman world as well as in Judaism; but with the difference that Jewish meals were never purely secular. The Hebrew Bible speaks of a "covenant of salt" (Num 18:19; 2 Chr 13:50), by which sharers in a meal become bound in solidarity. It was considered a heinous crime to betray one with whom a meal had been shared (Ps 41:10; Jn 13:18).

The family meal was marked by thanksgivings at the beginning and at the end. To begin the meal, the head of the household held a piece of bread and said a prayer: "Blessed are you, O Lord our God, King of the world, who bring forth bread from the earth." The bread was then broken into pieces and passed around to all the participants. At the end of the meal there was another thanksgiving, called *Birkat Ha-Mazon,* longer than the blessing at the beginning. It included a thanksgiving for the rich heritage of the land of Israel and the Law, in addition to a thanksgiving for the meal. On special occasions this would be over a cup of wine, but ordinarily wine was not used at daily meals.[1]

Festive Meals

In the first century A. D. there was a standard form for the Jewish festive meal, of which there were variations for special occasions. Our information about the format of this meal comes from rabbinic sources later than the New Testament, so it might not reflect precisely the practice in the time of Jesus. But what I will be using in the following reconstruction comes from the Tannaitic literature of the first two centuries A. D. and is thought to be fairly accurate for the New Testament period.[2] Three summarizing texts are known from this early rabbinic period in witnesses gathered for the Mishnah tractate Berakoth. They differ only with regard to the order of mixing wine and washing hands:

[1]See George Foot More, *Judaism in the First Centuries of the Christian Era: the Age of the Tannaim* (Cambridge: Harvard Univ., 1962) II, 216-217.

[2]I am following G.J. Dahr in "The Seder of Passover and the Eucharistic Words," *NovT 12* (1970) 181-202.

What is the order of the meal? The guests enter the house and sit on benches and on chairs until all have entered. They all enter and the servants give them water for their hands. Each one washes one hand. The servants mix for them the cup; each one says the benediction for himself. The servants bring them the appetizers; each one says the benediction for himself. The guests go up to the dining room and they recline, and the servants give them water for their hands; although they have washed one hand, they now wash both hands. The servants mix for them the cup; although they have said a benediction over the first cup, they say a benediction over the second. The servants bring them the dessert; although they said a benediction over the first one, they say a benediction over the second, and one says the benediction for all of them. He who comes after the third course has no right to enter.[3]

This description is written to clarify ritual details and, like the accounts of the Last Supper, is not a complete program, but it does illuminate the known framework of Jewish meals. The Jewish festive meal had three courses: hors d'oeuvres, main course, and dessert. For the first course, guests were seated in an anteroom separated from the main dining room. The text reflects a period when the anteroom was on the ground floor, the refectory in an upper chamber. The guests washed one hand, the one used for eating (without utensil). The wine was mixed with water; guests blessed their own food and drink. The hors d'oeuvres could be a variety of things, such as lettuce, radishes, cucumbers, fruit and cheese.

After the appetizers, the guests moved upstairs to the main dining room. Festive meals were usually eaten in a reclining position, though ordinary meals were taken sitting. The reclining posture was an influence from Greco-Roman practice and was strong enough to counterbalance even the clear instruction of the book of Exodus to eat the Passover meal standing (Ex 12:11).[4] At the beginning of the main course each

---

[3]T. Berakoth IV, 8. The other texts are Pal. Berakoth 10d and Babyl. Berakoth 43a.

[4]T. Barosse, "The Passover and the Paschal Meal," *Concilium* 40 (Dec, 1968) 17.

person washed both hands, because now they would be needed for the meal and other food served. There was usually "first water" for washing before eating, and "last water" afterward. Though it is not mentioned in the summary, the main course began with the same signal that initiated a family meal, the breaking of the bread by the host or head of the assembly, with the customary benediction mentioned above. Then as each kind of food appeared for the first time, the leader blessed it in the name of all. He dipped into the bowl first, and then all followed his example. The blessing of the wine is ambiguous in the text quoted above, but the other two rabbinic sources make it clear that the cup at the main meal was blessed by the leader for all, because they had now become a community: "Blessed are you, O Lord, our God, eternal king, who create the fruit of the wine." The cups were refilled during this course as needed, at which point the individual said a private blessing.

At the end of the main course, the servants removed the food and brought in the small final course, a "dessert" consisting of bread and salted items of food.[5] The benediction at this time was a lengthy thanksgiving for the meal and what it represented, an expansion of the ordinary grace, given by the leader in the name of all. On important occasions, solemnity was added by having this benediction recited over a third cup of wine, which was then passed around to all participants. This special cup of wine became known as the "cup of blessing," a term which Paul uses in 1 Corinthians 10:16.[6]

In summary, the typical Jewish festive meal followed this outline:

First Course (Hors d'oeuvres)
Washing of one hand.
First cup of wine with individual blessing.
Appetizers with individual blessings.
Main Course
Washing of both hands.
Breaking of the bread.

---

[5]Bahr, "The Seder," 198.

[6]Whether this was a technical term for the third cup during Paul's time is uncertain; the rabbinic references may be to a later period: *Ibid.*, 197, n. 4.

Second cup of wine with blessing by leader.
Sharing of meal.
Third Course (Dessert)
Bread and salted items.
Thanksgiving for meal.
(Occasionally: Third cup of wine, "cup of blessing," shared by participants.)

Passover Meal

Scholars who consider the Johannine chronology of Holy Week accurate usually understand the Last Supper as a Jewish festive meal of the kind just described. It was not a Passover meal as such but had Passover motifs because of the proximity of the feast; as today, a family Christmas meal may take place during the season rather than on the day itself. But this is not a settled issue, as we have seen. Several interpreters still consider the Last Supper to have been a Passover meal, and other Jewish meal forms are candidates as well.

The annual Passover meal was a unique observance but followed the general pattern of the regular Jewish festive meal.[7] Some of the significant differences were the special foods, the recitation of the *Haggadah* or story of God's salvation of the Hebrew people, and the addition of two cups of wine (for a total of four).[8] The rabbis later said that this ritual of four cups came from the four Hebrew words used in Exodus 6:6-7 to describe the delivery of Israel from Egypt (translated in RSV as "bring you out," "deliver you," "redeem you," "brought you out"), and that even a poor man should not receive less than four cups of wine on this great occasion.

The evening meal was usually taken in the late afternoon, but this time the meal began after the sunset which marked the beginning of the first day of Passover. The paschal lambs had been slaughtered earlier in the afternoon. The participants

---

[7] See Hayyim Schauss, *The Jewish Festivals: History and Observance* (New York: Schocken, 1962) 54-55.

[8] Bahr is mistaken in supposing that there were four formal cups at every festive meal; see L.N. Dembitz, "Seder," *Jewish Encyclopedia*, Vol II: 144.

blessed the first cup of wine as usual with the customary words. But there was also a special blessing for the sanctification of the day (*kiddush*). The order of these two blessings at the beginning of the Passover meal became a source of controversy between the schools of Rabbis Hillel and Shammai toward the end of the first century.[9]

The appetizers were blessed by the individual diners as usual. The menu for this night specified lettuce dipped in vinegar and salt water. After the breaking of the bread (signaling the beginning of the main course) came the blessing of the second cup of wine by the leader in the name of all. The food of the main course was unusual: unleavened bread, bitter herbs, *haroseth* (a mixture of nuts, fruit, and wine), and the paschal lamb. After the preparation of the second cup, the ritual called for the son to ask his father the important question: "Why is this night different from all other nights?" The complete form of the interrogation itemizes the unusual features of the Passover Meal:

For on all other nights we eat leavened or unleavened bread; tonight we eat only unleavened bread.

Every other night we eat all kinds of green vegetables; tonight, only bitter greens.

Every other night we eat meat either cooked, roasted, or stewed;

tonight, only roasted.

Every other night we dip once; tonight we dip twice.[10]

This was the cue for the father to respond with the paschal *Haggadah,* the story of Israel's slavery in Egypt and the deliverance by God's power. The participants were to see themselves as part of this saving action, not simply remembering the events as glories of the past. The narrative summary in Deuteronomy 26:5-8 was used as the starting point of this recitation; it lent itself well to making all feel a part of the deliverance: "A wandering Aramean was my father;... the Egyptians treated us harshly, and afflicted us, and laid upon us hard bondage;... and the Lord brought us out of Egypt with a

---

[9]M. Pesachim 10:2.

[10]M. Pesachim 10:4.

mighty hand and an outstretched arm." The narrative concluded with the recitation of the first part of the Hallel (Praise) Psalms.[11]

At the end of this main course a third cup of wine was mixed and a blessing said over it as a grace after meals. Usually dessert was brought in at this point, but this was forbidden at the Passover meal. The paschal lamb was the last food to be eaten during the main course; it was meant to be the "food which satiates," after which no food would be needed. A vestige of the third part of the regular festive meal remained in the mixing and blessing of a fourth cup[12] with the recitation of the second part of the Hallel psalms and a blessing "over the song."

Combining its special features with the standard program for a festive meal, the Passover meal may be outlined as follows (unique elements are marked with an asterisk):

First Course
Washing of one hand.
First cup of wine with individual blessing.
*Blessing for the sanctification of the day.
Appetizers with individual blessings.
Main Course
Washing of both hands.
Breaking of the bread.
Second cup of wine with blessing by leader.
*Sharing the meal: unleavened bread, paschal lamb.
*Questioning and *Haggadah.*
*First part of the Hallel psalms.
Thanksgiving for meal with
*third cup of wine, the "cup of blessing."
*Fourth cup of wine and the second part of the Hallel psalms.
*Blessing over the song.

[11]The Hallel Psalms (113-118) sing of the Lord's greatness and his victory for the lowly.

[12]It is not certain that there was a fourth cup of wine already in the time of Jesus.

Kiddush

When making his case for the paschal character of the Last Supper, Jeremias mentioned (and discarded) three other Jewish meal patterns which have been proposed as models for the Last Supper: the *Kiddush,* the *Haburah* meal, and the Essene meal. *Kiddush* ("sanctification") is the prayer by which the holiness of the Sabbath or a festival is proclaimed.When the first stars appear after sunset, the head of the household says the blessing at table over a cup of wine.[13] This is the blessing listed above during the first course of the Passover meal.

As Jeremias rightly notes, the *Kiddush* is not a meal at all, but a blessing at particular meals. The idea (influential around the turn of this century) that the Last Supper should be identified with the *Kiddush* arose because in later Jewish ritual the Sabbath *Kiddush* combined the blessing of the wine at the beginning of the meal with the breaking of bread. But at the time of Jesus there was no such combination.[14]

Haburah

A *Haburah* was a society of Pharisees united for the purpose of more precise and faithful observance of the Law. These groups, which originated in the second century B. C., met together for meals at which they supported one another in the renewal of their dedication.[15] Some exegetes, following Lietzmann, have proposed this *Haburah* meal as the context for the Last Supper. The most thorough statement of this position in English is by Dom Gregory Dix in *The Shape of the Liturgy.*[16] According to Dix, the members of a *Haburah* met for their meals weekly, generally on the eve of a Sabbath or feast. Their meal had the form common to the chief meal in

---

[13]I. Elbogen, "Kiddush," *Jewish Encyclopedia,* Vol. 7:483.

[14]Jeremias, *Eucharistic Words,* 27-28.

[15]S. Mendelsohn, "Haber," *Jewish Encyclopedia,* Vol. 6: 121, 124; H. Cazelles, "chābhar," *Theological Dictionary of the Old Testament,* Vol. 4: 197.

[16](Westminster: Dacre, 1945[2]) 50-70.

every Jewish household, but with more attention to ritual formalities. Jesus and his disciples would have formed a *Haburah,* with the difference from other such groups in the strength of their bond to the leader and in Jesus' independent attitude toward the religious authorities.

Jeremias contested the idea of the weekly *Haburah* meal, for which he claims there is no solid evidence in the sources. He does admit that the groups met together for meals but these were irregular "duty" meals (weddings, funerals, etc.) at which others were also present; these meals did not, therefore, have a special ritual or even "sacramental" meaning for the group.[17]

The argument about the *Haburah* meal, for which there is sparse and ambiguous evidence, may have narrowed the focus of the debate too much. Recent discussion has shifted attention to the more general category of Jewish festive meals. Dix foreshadowed this shift when he suggested that critics who disapprove of his argument for the *Haburah* meal might simply ignore that word and apply what he said to the formal evening meal of the Jewish household.[18]

Essene Meal

After the discovery of the Dead Sea Scrolls at Qumran in the late 1940's, much attention was given to possible connections between the Essene community and Jesus and his followers. The sect's documents show that the Essenes had daily communal meals. Were these meals the inspiration for the early Christian meals, and did they affect in any way the accounts of the Last Supper? Josephus describes the Qumran meal:

> They gather in a special hall into which no outsider is permitted to enter; neither would they themselves enter the refectory unless cleansed, as if it were some sacred precinct.

[17]Jeremias, *Eucharistic Words,* 30-31.

[18]Dix, *The Shape,* 50, n. 2. The lack of attention to these daily meals and particularly to the general category of the Jewish festive meal is a serious lack in Jeremias' presentation.

They take their seats without any uproar, then the baker serves to each commensal his bread, the cook puts before him a dish with but one foodstuff therein. The priest recites a prayer before the repast, and no one may touch it before the prayer is said. After the repast, he prays anew; all, both at the beginning and at the end return thanks to God, the bestower of the food which gives life.[19]

The Essenes' *Manual of Discipline* adds an element which makes the correspondence with the Last Supper more pointed: "When the table shall have been prepared for eating, or the wine for drinking, the priest shall first extend his hand to bless the first portions of bread or of wine" (1 QS VI:4-6). This mention of the wine and its blessing and distribution along with the bread is expanded in *The Rule for the Future Congregation of Israel:*

> If they happen to be foregathering for a common meal or to drink wine together, when the common board has been spread or the wine mixed for drinking, no one is to stretch out his hand for the first portion of the bread or wine prior to the priest. It is he who is to pronounce the blessing over the first portion of the bread or wine, and it is he that is first to stretch out his hand to the bread. After that, the anointed (king), a layman, is to stretch out his hand to the bread and after that the members of the community in general are to pronounce the blessing in order of rank. This rule is to obtain at all meals where there are ten or more men present.[20]

There is at first glance a similarity between the Essene meal and the Lord's Supper because of the mention of the bread and wine, the blessing and distribution by the priest. But any

---

[19] *The Jewish Wars* II, VIII, 5, in G. Vermes, *Discovery in the Judean Desert: The Dead Sea Scrolls and Their Meaning* (New York: Desclee, 1956), 54. There is a debate over whether these meals were religious rituals. For the affirmative position, see J. Gnilka, "Das Gemeinschaftsmahl der Essener," *BZ* 5 (1961) 39-55; for the negative, L.H. Schiffman, "Communal Meals at Qumran," *RevQ* 9 (1978) 569-73.

[20] *1 QSa II: 17-22,* in T.H. Gaster, *The Dead Sea Scriptures* (Garden City: Doubleday Anchor, 1956), 330.

influence either on the conduct of the Last Supper itself or the reports by the evangelists is very doubtful. It becomes even more doubtful when the Qumran meal is understood as a variation on the standard Jewish festive meal. Both the Qumran meal and the Last Supper are influenced by this standard format. A major difference of meaning between the Qumran meal and the Christian Eucharist is that the meals at Qumran anticipated the banquets of the messianic age to come; while the Christian ritual in addition celebrates the fulfillment in the presence of Jesus.

Todah

Recently scholars have begun to look to another form of sacred meal in their study of the early development of the Lord's Supper, a form that has deep roots in the Old Testament and was prominent in the time of Jesus. This is the *todah*, a thank offering by an individual or group which has experienced deliverance from sickness or other threat. The worshiper offers an animal in sacrifice in the midst of friends, and celebrates a new beginning with a meal offering (the *todah*) recounting the past troubles and the Lord's deliverance. The ritual is described in Leviticus 7:12-15:

> He shall offer with the thank offering unleavened cakes mixed with oil, unleavened wafers spread with oil, and cakes of fine flour well mixed with oil. With the sacrifice of his peace offerings for thanksgiving he shall bring his offering with cakes of leavened bread. And of such he shall offer one cake from each offering, as an offering to the Lord; it shall belong to the priest who throws the blood of the peace offerings. And the flesh of the sacrifice of his peace offerings for thanksgiving shall be eaten on the day of his offering; he shall not leave any of it till morning.

According to a recent study by Cesare Giraudo on the literary structure of the Eucharistic prayer, the *todah* observance is a celebration of the covenant.[21] It was especially important

_____

[21] See footnote 38 of Chapter 2. An earlier investigation along this line was made by

during post-exilic times and its influence appears in several psalms from that period which are witnesses to a spiritualizing of the idea of sacrifice. An unusual feature of the *todah* offering was the use of leavened bread; this normal bread of daily life emphasized the sacrifice of basic human nourishment by the one who had been rescued.[22]

The verb root of *todah* is an intensive form of the word *yadah* ("throw") which means "to give thanks" and contains the idea of "confession" both as praising God's goodness and expressing sorrow for past infidelities. A typical psalm using the *todah* pattern is the lament (recounting suffering and possibly personal sin) concluding with a prayer of thanksgiving. In Psalm 22, which Jesus prayed on the cross (Mk 15:34), the psalmist relates his miseries but ends on a positive note of praise, probably in the context of a thanksgiving offering in the temple: "In the midst of the congregation I will praise thee " (v. 22). Psalm 69 follows the same pattern of lament and praise, but also expresses the idea that God is better pleased with the thanksgiving sacrifice coming from the heart than from animal sacrifice:

> I will praise the name of God with a song;
> I will magnify him with thanksgiving.
> This will please the Lord more than an ox
> or a bull with horns and hoofs. (vv. 30-31)

As Gese comments, in these psalms we do not have so much a critique of animal sacrifice as an expression of the need for the total involvement of the person as the essence of sacrifice. The phrase which sums up this spirit is "sacrifice of praise" (Lev 7:12-19; Jer 17:26; Ps 50:14, 23).

With the *todah* as pattern, the Lord's Supper is the thank offering of the Risen Lord in which we participate. The saving death of Jesus is remembered, and salvation is proclaimed in the raising of the "cup of salvation" (Ps 116: 13). The old

Louis Ligier: "From the Last Supper to the Eucharist," in L. Sheppard, ed., *The New Liturgy* (London: Darton, Longman, & Todd, 1970) 113-50.

[22]Helmut Gese, "The Origin of the Lord's Supper," *Essays on Biblical Theology* (Minneapolis: Augsburg, 1981) 130.

covenant was established in a blood ceremony and so was the second. To share the meal of the sacrificial animal and the bread-offering renewed one's union with the God of the covenant. To share the bread and cup of the Lord's Supper renews one's share in the new covenant in Christ.

Several years before interest focused on the *todah* in tracing the development of the Eucharist, liturgical scholars began pursuing another channel to similar conclusions about its origins. Much has been written during the past twenty-five years about the relationship of the ritual of the Eucharist to the basic Jewish prayer form, the *berakah* (blessing).[23]

In the late 1950's, J.P. Audet argued that the Christian Eucharist is based on the Jewish "cultic *berakah*," and that besides *eulogein* (bless), two other Greek words, *exomologeisthai* and *eucharistein*, are equivalent translations of the Hebrew *barak* in late Old Testament literature.[24] Later study has concluded that Audet's identifications were too facile. The verb *eucharistein* (give thanks) is a proper Greek rendering for a Hebrew word used in Jewish worship, but the word is not *barak*.

Interest has focused on the *Birkat Ha-Mazon*, the Jewish grace after meals alluded to earlier. This prayer has three parts, a benediction (beginning with a form of *barak*), a thanksgiving (beginning with a form of *yadah*, the root of *todah*) and a supplication. A text of a *Birkat Ha-Mazon* traceable to the early second century A.D. reads as follows:

> I. Blessed art Thou, O Lord, our God, King of the Universe, Who feedest the whole world with goodness, with grace, and with mercy. Blessed art Thou, O Lord, Who feedest all. II. We thank Thee, O Lord, our God, that Thou hast caused us to inherit a goodly and pleasant land, the covenant, the Torah, life and food. For all these things we thank Thee and praise Thy name for ever and ever. Blessed art Thou, O Lord, for the land and for the food.

[23]See Talley, "From *Berakah* to *Eucharistia*."

[24]"Literary Forms and Contents of a Normal *Eucharistia* in the First Century," *Studia Evangelica, TU* 73 (Berlin, 1959), 643-662.

III. Have mercy, O Lord, our God, on Thy people Israel, and on Thy city Jerusalem, and on Thy Temple and Thy dwelling-place and on Zion Thy resting-place, and on the great and holy sanctuary over which Thy name was called, and the kingdom of the dynasty of David mayest Thou restore to its place in our days, and build Jerusalem soon. Blessed are Thou, O Lord, who buildest Jerusalem.[25]

Talley argues that this prayer form substantiates the originality of Mark/ Matthew tradition's use of *eulogēsas* ("blessed") in the bread-word (Mk 14:22; Mt 26:26), and explains the use of *eucharistēsas* "gave thanks") in the cup-word (Mk 14:23; Mt 26:27). Over the bread Jesus would have recited a *berakah* (accurately translated by *eulogein*), corresponding to part one of the *Birkat Ha-Mazon*. Over the cup at the conclusion of the meal (after another short *berakah*), he then began the prayer which corresponds to part two (beginning with an intensive form of *yadah* meaning "to give thanks"—accurately rendered by *eucharistein*). This part of the prayer opens up the possibility of remembering the saving acts of God, a focus which was to become central to the Christian Eucharastic Prayer.

The use of *eucharistein* in the Supper accounts is thus rooted directly in the Jewish prayer tradition, but comes from the Hebrew *yadah* rather than from *barak*. Because the *yadah*-prayer was more open to liturgical expansion in terms of *anamnēsis* (remembering God's mighty deeds), it better served the needs of the Lord's Supper. According to Talley, the prayer's opening *yadah* verb "proved determinative for Paul and Luke and Justin and the entire tradition, *he gave thanks.*" Thus by the time of the Didache (c. 100), the Christian cultic meal was called *eucharistia.* [26]

---

[25]The translation of Louis Finkelstein, "The Birkat Ha-Mazon," *JQR* 19 (1928-29) 215-216, reproduced in Talley, "From *Berakah* to *eucharistia*," 121-122.

[26]*Ibid.,* 124. The transition from *eulogein* to *eucharistein* appears also in the multiplication accounts. In the parallels of the First Feeding, the Synoptics all have *eulogēsen* (Mt 14:19, Mk 6:41; Lk 9:16), but John has *eucharistēsas* (Jn 6:11). For the Second Feeding, Matthew and Mark describe Jesus' invocation over the bread and fish by the verb *eucharistēsas* (Mt 15:36; Mk 8:6).

Summary

The sparseness of the accounts of the Last Supper has made it difficult to reconstruct the framework with which to interpret the words and actions of Jesus. Within Judaism the meal was an important social and religious ritual with several variations. Besides the daily family meal, there was a pattern for a more festive meal which also provided a general outline for particular observances, such as the Passover meal. This meal began with the customary breaking of the bread and had two formal cups of wine, but on especially significant occasions provided for a third cup, the "cup of blessing," shared by the participants. Besides this, the Passover meal format called for an interpretative statement by the leader.

In searching for the context of the Last Supper, various Jewish meal rituals have been considered over the years, among them the *Kiddush*, the *Haburah* meal and the Essene meal. These forms have largely been abandoned as candidates; today the discussion revolves around the general category of the Jewish festive meal, or to the specific format used for the Passover meal. Recently, in investigating the development of the Lord's Supper, attention has been drawn to the *todah* meal of thank offering and the *todah* theme contained in the Jewish benediction after meals.

4

The Accounts of the Last Supper

Our review of the scholarly discussion about the biblical narratives and about the Jewish meal tradition in the time of Jesus provides us with a context to take a direct look at the Supper accounts. The first task is to raise the question that has already introduced itself several times: what kind of meal was the Last Supper?

All four of the Gospels relate the Last Supper to the Jewish Passover. In the Synoptics, the rubrics for "preparing to eat the passover" are quite specific (Mk 14:12, 16; Mt 26:17,19; Lk 22:8,13). The Supper is a Passover meal. John, on the other hand, places the meal "before the feast of the Passover" (Jn 13:1); Jesus' death the following day coincides with the sacrifice of the lambs in the temple before the Passover meal. There is no reference to the Passover in Paul's account of the Lord's Supper (1 Cor 11:23-26). In fact, as mentioned earlier, the New Testament never interprets the Eucharist in the light of the Passover.[1]

Solutions to the question of the nature of the Last Supper fall into three categories. 1) Both chronologies are correct. The Supper was a Passover meal but was celebrated at an alternate time because of differences in liturgical calendars. 2) The Synoptic chronology is correct: it was a Passover meal, but John changed the chronology in order to make the death of Jesus take place at the time of the paschal sacrifice, which

---

[1]Some have seen a paschal reference in Paul's mention of the "cup of blessing" (1 Cor 10:16), but this is inconclusive because other meals had a cup of blessing.

conforms to his theology of Jesus as the Lamb of God. 3) John's chronology is correct: it was not a Passover meal.

One harmonizing theory, espoused recently by Marshall, has already been discussed in Chapter 2. According to this, Jesus was following the Pharisaic practice of observing the Passover one day earlier than the Sadducees. Jeremias' criticism of this theory as "wholly conjectural" still stands.[2] Another well-known harmonizing proposal of recent times was made by Annie Jaubert.[3] According to her theory, Jesus was following a solar calendar (mentioned at Qumran and in the Book of Jubilees) rather than the official lunar calendar of Jerusalem. This calendar divided the year into four quarters of 91 days each, with each quarter beginning on the same day, Wednesday. The Passover meal always fell on a Tuesday. Thus, Jesus celebrated the Passover meal with his disciples on Tuesday evening according to the calendar used by the Essenes. He was arrested later that night, tried and condemned during the next two days, and put to death on Friday. Jaubert found this chronology of Passion week verified in the Syriac Didascalia of the early third century and in a letter of Epiphanius of Salamis of the middle of the fourth century.

The main problem with this theory, as with the one described above, is that we have no evidence (earlier than the Syriac Didascalia) that Jesus followed any but the official calendar of the temple priests. Had Jesus done so, it would have given the leaders a prime opportunity to question him on his observance (the solar calendar would have been considered illegal), but there is no record of that in the Gospels. The harmonizing theories remain hypothetical.

The classic case for the accuracy of the Synoptics' report of the Last Supper as a Passover meal has been made by Jeremias. His arguments are, briefly, the following: 1) Jewish law demanded that the Passover meal be eaten in Jerusalem; Jesus went to special effort to hold the meal in Jerusalem, even though he had been staying at Bethany. 2) The ready availability of the room fits with the Jewish custom of special

[2]*Eucharistic Words*, 23-24.
[3]See Chapter 2, note 33.

hospitality for the Passover meal. 3) The meal was eaten at night, but ordinary meals were eaten in late afternoon. 4) Jesus ate the meal with a small number of intimate companions, which was typical of the Passover. 5) The participants reclined at table, a sign that the meal was special; the ordinary posture at a meal was sitting. 6) Levitical purity was required at the paschal meal; this is implied at the Last Supper by the exchange about "no need to wash" (Jn 13:10). 7) Jesus broke bread during the course of the meal rather than at the beginning. The Passover meal was the only one in which the serving of a dish preceded the breaking of bread.

8) The participants drank wine, which was required at the Passover meal. The ordinary drink with meals was water. 9) Jesus used red wine (conjectured from the comparison with blood), which was required for the meal by the rabbis. 10) When Judas left, some of the disciples thought he was going to make purchases. He would not have needed to do this at night, unless it were near the beginning of the Passover, when no business was permitted. 11) Other disciples assumed Judas was to give something to the poor, which was customary on Passover night. 12) The meal ended with the singing of a hymn, which corresponds to the recitation of the second part of the Hallel psalms at the end of the Passover meal. 13) Jesus did not go out to Bethany but to the Mount of Olives after the meal; the night of the Passover had to be spent in Jerusalem. 14) The utterance of words of interpretation over the bread and wine corresponds to the *Haggadah* interpretation in the Passover meal ritual.[4]

Léon-Dufour is a strong opponent of the position that the Last Supper was a Passover meal. He gives a point by point refutation of Jeremias' arguments in his recent book (omitting numbers 2, 6, 10, 11, 13, which he claims hardly pertain to the question).[5] To summarize the responses of Léon-Dufour: 1) Circumstantial argument: Jesus may have had other reasons for holding the meal in Jerusalem. 3) The Passover meal was not the only solemn meal eaten at night. 4) The small number

[4] *Eucharistic Words*, 42-61

[5] *Le partage du pain*, 350-351

of participants could have been for other reasons. 5) Jeremias himself gives many examples of other occasions when Jews reclined at meals. 7) In other solemn meals, as well, the breaking of the bread was preceded by the eating of hors d'oeuvres. 8) Wine was not the ordinary drink, but neither was its table use limited to the Passover meal. 9) The rabbinic rule about the color of the wine is from a later time. 12) Singing at the close of a meal was also the practice of the Therapeutae of Egypt (an ascetical Jewish community). 14) Jesus' words of interpretation were not about the past (as was the Passover *Haggadah*), but a prophetic explanation of his action.[6]

Besides the obvious difficulty of John's chronology, the Passover meal theory has to deal also with the problem of feverish activity on the first day of Passover (arrest, trials, purchases, execution, opening a new tomb, etc.). Though Jeremias furnishes evidence that none of these activities was absolutely unforeseen on the Passover, we could expect some mention of conflict with Passover observance in these activities, but there is none.[7] Further, aside from the reports in the Synoptic Gospels, there is nothing in the New Testament to cause us to think that the Last Supper was a Passover meal. If the exegetes are correct who consider Luke 22:15-18 independent of Mark 14:25, then there are two independent witnesses to the Synoptic tradition. But if the Lucan text is an expansion of the Marcan, then Mark is the sole witness. The second evangelist, writing possibly from Rome for a Gentile audience, may not have had an eyewitness source for this detail, which could then be the product of a confused transmission through non-Jewish believers.

Jeremias' careful presentation of his case served the purpose of focusing the debate about the nature of the Last Supper. After these years of discussion, the best evidence is that the Last Supper was not the Passover meal of that year but a festive Jewish meal organized by Jesus as a farewell dinner when he recognized that official opposition to him was

---

[6]Léon-Dufour's response is weakest on arguments 12 and 14, but even these remain inconclusive arguments.

[7]See arguments for the reliability of John's chronology in R.E. Brown, *The Gospel According to John XIII-XXI* (AB 29A; Garden City: Doubleday, 1970), 556.

mounting at an ever accelerating peace. He foresaw the likelihood that he might be prevented from celebrating the Passover meal with his disciples the following night because of imprisonment or worse. The meal had paschal overtones because of its proximity to the feast and because of Jesus' reference to Passover and covenant themes. The unusual solemnity he gave it in terms of his mission and his relationship to these intimate friends abetted the Passover association in the tradition. But the Supper is completely explainable within the typical outline of the festive Jewish meal.

The Supper Accounts

The chart of the four Supper accounts makes their similarities visible at a glance. Even a slight probing reveals many dissimilarities, however, and the improbability of being able to write the script of the Last Supper from these accounts. Three (the Synoptics) are in the form of narrative history and the other (1 Corinthians) is a liturgical formulary; but all, not only that of Paul, have been influenced by community liturgy through their transmission during the early years of the Church. But there is enough convergence to make it possible to know essentially what Jesus did and what he meant by it. The radical skepticism of the recent past has no basis any more.

The earliest of the four documents is First Corinthians, in which St. Paul, writing in the mid-50's, reminds the community at Corinth of what he had passed on to them when he first came to them about five years earlier. What he transmits about the Lord's Supper is a fixed formula (similar to the creed a few chapters later: 1 Cor 15:3-5). As such, it is pared to the essentials. Paul himself had learned this account of the Last Supper in the community at Antioch in the mid-40's. It had been translated into Greek from an account of Palestinian origin. Even though the account comes to us in a liturgically-edited form, it takes us back to within a decade of the Last Supper.

Luke's account was written thirty or forty years later, and at first sight seems to be dependent on Paul's account, which it resembles. But there are signs that it is not. Luke omits the

Mt. 26:26-29	Mark 14:22-25	Luke 22:15-20	1 Cor. 11:23-26
		[15]And he said to them,	[23]The Lord Jesus on the night
		'I have earnestly desired	when he was betrayed
		to eat this passover with you	took-bread,
		before I suffer;	[24]and gave thanks,
		[16]for I tell you	broke it
		I shall not eat it	
		until	and said,
		it is fulfilled	
		in the kingdom of God.'	
		[17]And he took a cup,	
		and when he had given thanks	
		he said,	
		'Take this,	
		and divide it among yourselves;	
		[18]for I tell you that from now on	
		I shall not drink	
		of the fruit of the vine	
		until	
		the kingdom of God comes.	
[26]Now as they were eating,	[22]And as they were eating,	[19]And	
Jesus took bread,	he took bread,	he took bread,	
and blessed,	and blessed,	gave thanks,	
and broke it,	and broke it,	broke it	
and gave it to the disciples	and gave it to them,	and gave it to them,	
and said,	and said,	saying,	
'Take, eat;	'Take;		

this is my body.

27And he took a cup,

and when he had given thanks
he gave it to them,

saying,
'Drink of it, all of you:
28for this is
my blood
of the covenant,
which is poured out
for many
for the forgiveness of sins.

29I tell you
I shall not drink
again
of this fruit of the vine
until that day when
I drink it new with you
in my Father's kingdom.'

---

this is my body.

23And he took a cup,
and when he had given thanks
he gave it to them,
and they all drank of it.
24And he said to them,

'This is
my blood
of the covenant,
which is poured out
for many.

25Truly, I tell you
I shall not drink
again
of the fruit of the vine
until that day when
I drink it new
in the kingdom of God.'

'This is my body
which is given for you.
Do this in remembrance of me.'

20And the cup likewise
after supper

saying,

'This cup is
the new covenant
in my blood
which is poured out
for you.

'This is my body
which is   for you.
Do this in remembrance of me.'

25Likewise also the cup
after supper,

saying,

'This cup is
the new covenant
in my blood.

Do this,
as often as you drink it,
in remembrance of me.'

vs 26?

second remembrance-word, which is hardly explainable if Luke is using Paul. Luke also adds to the cup-word the phrase "which is poured out for you." Luke does not otherwise have an expiation theology.[8] Doubtless he is incorporating this phrase, which jars with his theological preferences, from a received tradition, perhaps Mark at this point. But if Luke had the warrant of Paul's omission of the phrase, he would most likely not have incorporated it. Both Luke and Paul have eschatological sayings, but there seems to be no dependency either way. The best interpretation of the evidence is that Paul and Luke were working independently from the same source, the Antiochean liturgical tradition; the differences between them show the influence of other sources.

Mark, written around 70, is closer in time to First Corinthians than is Luke, but shows no signs of being influenced by Paul's narrative. The Semitic flavor of Mark's account supports the argument of Jeremias and Pesch for an early Palestinian origin. Mark's version is followed closely by Matthew, whose changes are relatively easy to explain in terms of the evangelist's writing style, his theology and the liturgical usage of his community.[9] He changes the frequency of *kai* (and) in Mark from six to four, and makes specific that Jesus gave the bread to the disciples (*mathētais*: an important word for Matthew). Mark has the disciples drink of the cup before Jesus' word of interpretation. Matthew edits out this awkwardness. Matthew's theology of the death of Jesus as an atoning sacrifice explains the addition of "poured out . . . for the forgiveness of sins" (Mt 26:28). Matthew's narrative has a significance of its own within his Gospel (Stage Three), but it does not contribute independently to the search for the earlier tradition (Stages One and Two).

Neither Paul/Luke nor Mark can claim primitiveness completely. Both show some signs of earliness and others of lateness. Signs of primitive data in Mark are the drinking of the cup before the words of interpretation (14:23-24), the

---

[8]See R.H. Fuller, "*Luke and the Theologia Crucis*," 214-220, and Jerome Kodell, "*Luke's Theology of the Death of Jesus*," 221-230, in Daniel Durken, ed., *Sin, Salvation, and the Spirit* (Collegeville: Liturgical Press, 1979).

[9]J.P. Meier, *Matthew* (Wilmington: Glazier, 1980), 318-319.

phrase "for many" (v. 24), and the eschatological promise (v. 25). Liturgical usage would have transferred the words to precede the drinking, as in the other accounts, but the reverse process is unlikely. "For many" is a Semiticism which could have been understood by Greek readers in a partitive sense, but in Hebrew it does not mean some as opposed to all; the meaning here is everyone except Jesus.[10]

Evidence of the secondary quality of parts of the Marcan narrative are the indefinite rubric "As they were eating"(v. 22), and the streamlining and paralleling of the bread and cup actions. The vague rubric shows that by this time the memory of details had faded. From Mark's text it would seem that the bread-cup actions were continuous, as in the liturgy. But we know that these actions could be separated in the Jewish meal; the Paul/Luke tradition says that the cup came "after supper."[11] In Mark's version, "This is my body" has been paralleled by "This is my blood . . . ," a natural development for cultic use.[12]

Signs of primitiveness in the Paul/Luke tradition are generally contrasts to the Marcan data. Besides the common eschatological emphasis (Mk 14:25; 1 Cor 11:26; Lk 22:15-18), "This is the cup" comes from a stage before the liturgy had brought the bread-and-cup words into parallel, and the meal between the bread and cup better reflects the pattern of Jewish festive (and Passover) meals. Later developments are evident in the change from "for many" to "for you," which was an application to later worshipers in the Greek-speaking world. Paul's naming of Jesus as "Lord" (11:23) is an insight of post-Easter faith. The use of *eucharistēsas* (gave thanks: 1 Cor

---

[10]See G.S. Sloyan, "'Primitive' and 'Pauline' Concepts of the Eucharist," *CBQ* 23 (1961), 5. The translation "for the many" might make this point more clearly. The same problem with translating a Semiticism still plagues the Church in the charge by some groups that the wording of the new Eucharistic Prayers, "will be shed for you and *for all*" is a mistranslation of the *pro multis effundetur* of the Roman Canon (Eucharistic Prayer I).

[11]The connection of the Lord's Supper with a regular meal still existed in the Corinthian community, as we know from 1 Cor 11:20-21, but apparently by that time the Lord's Supper followed the meal.

[12]By the mid-second century, the Roman liturgy had shortened the cup-word simply to "This is my blood," making the parallel exact: Justin, *I Apol.*, 66.

11:24; Lk 22:19) instead of *eulogēsas* (blessed: Mk 14:22; Mt 26:26), the ordinary rendering of the Hebrew *barak* in the Greek Old Testament, indicates the secondary quality of the Paul/Luke tradition in the bread parallels.[13]

Any effort to reconstruct the course of events at the Last Supper also has to deal with a major textual question in Luke. The Lucan narrative tells of two cups, one before and one after the bread. But there are a few ancient manuscripts which omit the verses describing the second cup.[14] After the words "This is my body" in 22:19, these manuscripts proceed immediately to verse 21 and the mention of the betrayer. The effect of this omission is to eliminate the double-cup discrepancy, but it leaves an order of cup-bread instead of bread-cup as in the other narratives.[15] Further, it removes from Luke the expiation motif and the mandate to repeat what Jesus has done.

Why is this shorter text with its few witnesses given any consideration? The arguments gathered by B.M. Metzger are these: a) Generally in textual criticism the shorter reading is preferred, because the tendency is to add rather than to subtract in transmission. b) Verses 19b-20 are similar to 1 Corinthians 11: 24b-25 and may have been incorporated from the earlier writing. c) Verses 19b-20 contain several non-Lucan linguistic features. I would add that the expiation theme is not characteristic of Luke. In favor of the longer text are: a) It is represented in all the ancient text-types of both East and West, while the shorter reading is found only in part of the Western tradition. b) It is easier to imagine the scribal elimination of the second cup than its addition. c) Some manuscripts may have been circulated in abbreviated form to keep information about the Eucharist away from outsiders who might profane it.[16]

---

[13] Mark/Matthew have *eucharistēsas* in connection with the cup, where Paul/Luke mention neither blessing nor thanksgiving. Luke has *eucharistēsas* over his first cup (22:17).

[14] These are the Greek manuscript D (fifth century), and five Latin manuscripts from the fourth, fifth and seventh centuries. Some other Latin and Syriac witnesses have compromise texts.

[15] The cup-bread order is found in Didache IX, 1-3.

[16] B.M. Metzger, *A Textual Commentary on the Greek New Testament* (London: United Bible Societies, 1971) 173-177.

There are still critics who maintain the originality of the shorter text, as we saw in Chapter 2, but the majority now accept the longer text. The strongest argument in its favor is the antiquity and breadth of the texts which contain the longer text. The presence of non-Lucan features in the questionable verses can be viewed as another sign of Luke's known reverence for tradition, which might be expected especially in passages with such impact on the life of the Christian community.

The traditions have preserved as the core of what Jesus said and did at the Last Supper the distribution of the bread and the wine with the words, "This is my body . . . this is my blood." A spectrum of interpretations of these gestures and words is possible, and their meaning is one of the division points among Christians. They need to be viewed against the background of Hebrew prophetic symbols. For us, the word "symbolic" is often used in contradiction to "real," and a symbol is an action or object that stands metaphorically for something else. To the Hebrew mind, symbols were realities in their own right, the prophetic word made visible. The symbolic action in some sense brought the event into existence.[17]

Jesus was saying "This is myself": by sharing this meal with you I am bringing you into an intimate relationship with myself. We cannot tell anymore whether the remembrance command (present in Paul/Luke, absent in Mark/Matthew) was uttered by Jesus himself or was added later. But its presence in some of the accounts is merely a confirmation of the mandate to continue doing what Jesus had done, which the the practice of the Church indicates was an early and unchallenged conviction.[18] This repetition of the rite after the Last Supper is always based on faith in the resurrection. Sharing the bread and wine unites us to Jesus as he is now, the risen Lord in glory.

The meaning of Jesus' words and actions, if it could be thought ambiguous in the institution accounts, is brought out

[17]Bruce Vawter, "Introduction to Prophetic Literature," *JBC* 12:23. See N.A. Beck, "The Last Supper as an Efficacious Symbolic Act," *JBL* 89 (1970) 192-198.

[18]The idea of the repetition of the Supper in the life of the Church is also involved in the promise in Lk 22:16, 18.

clearly in other New Testament references. Paul asks the rhetorical question of the Corinthians: "The cup of blessing which we bless, is it not a participation in the blood of Christ?" The bread which we break, is it not a participation in the body of Christ?" (I Cor 10:16). This sharing brings us into intimate unity with Christ, and in his life we are bonded into one (v. 17). Eating this bread and drinking this cup unworthily makes one guilty of "profaning the body and blood of the Lord" (11:27). Jesus' words in the bread of life discourse in the Fourth Gospel seem to be a Johannine version of the words of institution: "The bread which I shall give for the life of the world is my flesh" (Jn 6:51).[19] The two disciples at Emmaus recognized Jesus in the breaking of the bread (Lk 24:30-31). Passages like these reflect the community's understanding that Jesus' words at the Last Supper were meant with the realism of prophetic symbol, and that he would confirm them with his presence at each re-enactment of the Lord's Supper.

The benediction over the bread (blessing or praising God for the gift of bread), the breaking of the bread and the distribution to the meal participants—these actions, we have seen, were the ordinary way to begin the Jewish meal. What was different was the interpretation, "This is my body." The phrase "which is (given) for you" in Paul/Luke is probably a later clarification, under the influence of the cup-word, of the truth implied by the sharing of the bread identified as Jesus' body.

It seems clear that the cup spoken of in all four accounts as coming after the bread was not the second cup of wine (accompanying the main course), but was the third cup, always present in a Passover meal and also common for other festive meals.[20] This identification is supported by "after supper" in Paul/Luke and by the mention of the "cup of blessing" in 1 Corinthians 10:16. This third cup already expressed a special solidarity among the participants, and was appropriate for

---

[19]See R.E. Brown, *The Gospel According to John I-XII* (AB 29; Garden City: Doubleday, 1966), 282-285.

[20]D. Cohn-Sherbok's argument that Jesus blessed the fourth cup depends on two questionable assumptions: that the Last Supper was a Passover meal, and that there was a fourth cup in Jesus' time; "A Jewish Note on *to pōterion tēs eulogias,*" *NTS* 27 (1981) 704-709.

Jesus' words about a covenant bond. Mark is more accurate in using *eulogēsas* ("blessed") over the breaking of the bread and *eucharistēsas* ("gave thanks") with the cup, which marked the thanksgiving after the meal.

I regard Pesch's fundamental position as correct: that the Last Supper accounts take us back not merely to the interpretation of the Church but to Jesus' own understanding of his death and the meaning it gave to the farewell meal. Mark is accurate in the brevity of the bread-word, which simply introduced a new element into the familiar ritual and served as a harbinger of the more complete interpretation to come after the meal in the context of the *Birkat Ha-Mazon*.

But the cup formula in Mark is secondary. "This is my blood" smooths out the parallel with "This is my body." The phrase "of the covenant" is included awkwardly: literally "This is the blood of me of the covenant."[21] The Paul/Luke form of the cup-word, "This is the new covenant in my blood" has more marks of originality. The clear allusion to the Sinai covenant in Mark's version is only a clarification of the reference that is always there in a mention of covenant blood. The conjunction of "new covenant," which Jeremiah meant as completely interior, with "blood" is too shocking to be secondary. Covenant blood is always sacrificial blood. We find here the germ of the legitimate development of the sacrifice terminology found in the Letter to the Hebrews (9:26; 10:12) and later in the Church; and the source as well of the concept of the Eucharist as "unbloody sacrifice."[22]

The final interpretative phrase expressing the idea of expiation is present in both Mark and Paul/Luke (or better, in the common tradition Paul and Luke used for the bread-word). Pesch is correct on the originality of the Marcan placing of the formulation, ". . . which is poured out for many" with the cup. This statement along with the ransom-word (Mk 10:45) and other New Testament references to Isaiah 53 point to an authentic tradition of Jesus' self-understanding as the

---

[21] Bultmann, *Theology* I, 146.

[22] The idea of communion as sharing in the sacrifice is present in 1 Cor 10:18-21. See the discussion in Sverre Aalen, "Das Abendmahl als Opfermahl im Neuen Testament," *NT* 6 (1963) 131-134.

Servant of God. Jesus foresees his death as bringing atonement and inaugurating the new covenant foretold by Jeremiah. This meal is a prophetic symbol of that achievement.

Though the eschatological saying in Mark 14:25 and Luke 22: 15-20 are related, the relationship is not one of dependency by Mark on Luke, but, as Schürmann rightly demonstrates, both are independently witnesses to a common source.[23] In Mark's placing of the saying, Jesus' vow of abstinence follows the meal and will remain in force until the messianic fulfillment. Jesus will not share the banquet again until after his death and resurrection. In Luke, the vow of abstinence takes place before the meal. This is most likely where it was situated in Luke's source rather than a rearrangement by the Evangelist intended to make the Last Supper a meal of the realized kingdom.[24] Luke's first cup is correctly positioned according to the Jewish meal format, and the eschatological saying is connected to it. The extra cup is awkward and would not have been introduced by later tradition. It seems more likely that Mark, having received the isolated "fruit of the wine" saying, connected it to the later cup.

Summary

Though the Last Supper was not the Passover meal of that year, the proximity of the feast added Passover overtones to the meal which left their mark in the memory of the Church. The Eucharist is not interpreted in light of the Passover, but elsewhere Jesus' victory is spoken of as an exodus (Lk 9:31), and Paul refers to "Christ our Passover" (1 Cor 5:7). Jesus himself may have implied a comparison to the Passover lamb in referring to his blood being poured out. This theme is developed by John (Jn 19:36).

None of the Supper accounts is uniquely original. All have been affected by community tradition, especially liturgical

---

[23]Schürmann, *Der Paschamahlbericht*, 123.

[24]But see Dennis M. Sweetland, "The Lord's Supper and the Lukan Community," *BTB* 13 (1983) 23-27.

practice. Mark's account (followed by Matthew) has its roots in an early Palestinian tradition, while Paul and Luke reflect the liturgical tradition of Antioch. Both are traceable to the first decade of the Church.

The Supper scene is not a creation of the community. The accounts reveal Jesus' own understanding of his death and his meaning and purpose at the Last Supper. By a prophetic symbolic action, Jesus invited his disciples into an intimate relationship through the sharing of the bread and wine. This sharing of life would be reiterated later in community meals in the Lord's presence. By allusions to the Old Testament, Jesus identified himself as the Isaian Servant of God giving his life in atonement, and interpreted his actions as the inauguration of the new covenant foreseen by Jeremiah.

Part Two
Interpretations

5

The Eucharist of Paul

Paul is our earliest witness to Christian eucharistic practice and understanding, taking us into the Corinthian celebration of the Lord's Supper in the mid-50's. We have seen that all the authors of the New Testament books we are studying were heirs of an earlier, often complicated development. Paul does not necessarily present the earliest Christian practice or the earliest interpretation. But the antiquity of Paul's writing on the Eucharist does demand for it an important place in the study of its meaning and practice from the earliest times. This is heightened by the fact that Paul was explicitly concerned with passing on the tradition he had received from authentic sources (1 Cor 11:23).

It is commonly understood that Paul is presenting the liturgical practice as he had learned it in Antioch, where he had arrived at the summons of Barnabas in the early 40's (Acts 11:25-26). Acts presents Antioch as the center of the missionary movement of which Paul was eventually the leader. This was his home base. Though the historical reliability of Acts may be questioned in particulars, this Antiochene focus is substantiated by Paul's statement that Peter "came to Antioch" (Gal 2:11), implying that Antioch was Paul's own community. In First Corinthians 11:23, Paul says that he received his information about the Eucharist "from the Lord." This does not mean that he learned it in a private revelation or personal appearance of Jesus, but that he had learned it in the living Christian community, in which the risen Lord was present (1 Cor 6:15; 12:27).[1]

[1]See Hans Conzelmann, *1 Corinthians* (Hermeneia; Philadelphia: Fortress, 1975),

Paul's references to the Eucharist come only in First Corinthians. We presume that Paul brought the same liturgical practice to all the communities he founded, but his other correspondence shows no evidence of this. In First Corinthians the issue of the Eucharist is raised because of community problems which impinged on its meaning and practice. It has often been observed that, had the Corinthians been a more docile and disciplined community, we would not know whether or not the Pauline communities had the Eucharist. The Eucharist is mentioned at two places in First Corinthians: in 10:14-22, where Paul compares the Christian Eucharist to pagan and Jewish sacrifices; and in 11:17-34, where Paul is dealing with abuses in the Corinthian celebration of the Eucharist.

Sharing the Cup and the Bread (1 Cor 10:14-22)

The first clear reference to the Eucharist is Paul's rhetorical question: "The cup of blessing which we bless, is it not a participation in the blood of Christ? The bread which we break, is it not a participation in the body of Christ? Because there is one bread, we who are many are one body, for we all partake of the same loaf" (vv 16-17). Paul is referring to a concept he feels will be familiar to the Corinthians; they know this truth, but have only a superficial understanding of it (see 3:16). "Cup of blessing" probably refers to the third cup of wine at a Jewish festive meal.[2] In the Christian Eucharist this cup has been given a new meaning as a sharing in the blood of Christ. Paul mentions it before the bread here, not to indicate an order different from the traditional one, but so that he can develop the answer to his question in connection with the one loaf.

Paul's statement about the Eucharist here is not free-

---

196. Luke shares with Paul the same general tradition of the Last Supper. As noted above, there are some differences which make it more likely that both were influenced by a common source rather than that Luke (writing about thirty years later) is copying from Paul.

[2]See above, Chapter 3.

standing, though its connection with the context is not clear at first sight. He seems to pass from one issue to another without logical progression: from a warning about temptations (10:12-13) to an admonition against idol worship (vv 14-15) to the question about the meaning of the cup and the bread (vv 16-17). But these sentences are embedded within the argument of a section composed of Chapters 8-10, which has a frame dealing with the issue of meat offered to idols (8:1-13; 10:23-33) and a central section drawing implications from the principles enunciated in that discussion.

The Corinthians were divided over the question of eating meat which had been offered to idols. Parts of the pagan sacrificial animals were sold in the common market to raise funds for the upkeep of the temple and the salary of the priests. One group of Christians said that eating the meat was equivalent to participating in the pagan cult; while others maintained that it meant nothing since idols don't really exist. Paul responds by telling those who have no scruples about the meat (the "strong") that love calls them to sacrifice their rights for the sake of those with scruples (the "weak"). "If food is a cause of my brother's falling, I will never eat meat, lest I cause my brother to fall" (8:13). In the central section, Paul develops the idea of a loving sacrifice of rights, using himself as an example (9:1-27) of one who "made myself a slave to all" (v 19); and then refers to the overconfidence which may come when one relies on personal rights and superior knowledge (10:1-22). The statement on the Eucharist is part of the warning about overconfidence.

The Corinthians knew that sharing the cup and the bread brought a real participation in the body and blood of Christ. The word for "participation" is *koinōnia*, more than social fellowship: the saving call in Christ brings the believer into a new mode of existence which plunges one into a sharing of life with the Lord and with other participants. The sharing is not a metaphor but a reality, and the Corinthians know it. Jerome Murphy-O'Connor points out that this real participation in the body and blood of Christ is possible only if the bread and wine are in fact the body and blood of Christ. "The concept of spiritual communion was unknown to the Jews, and a share in the sacrifice was possible only through physical consumption of the flesh of the victim."[3]

To clinch his point, Paul refers to the Jewish belief that partaking of the sacrificial animals was a way of achieving union with God and to the similar understanding of pagans with regard to idol offerings. The "strong" at Corinth based their case for eating idol offerings on the principle that idols don't exist, a point that Paul confirms, and conclude that the eating of meat that has been offered to them is meaningless, a point that Paul denies. He contends that such participation lays them open to the demonic forces behind pagan worship: "You cannot drink the cup of the Lord and the cup of demons" (v 21). In these arguments, Paul simply shows the Corinthians the implications of their own Eucharistic belief, and in doing so opens up to us, as an aside, the early Christian understanding of the Eucharist. The Corinthians knew that partaking of the Eucharistic bread and cup was meaningless if it did not reinforce their union with the Lord Jesus.[4]

Another problem plaguing the Corinthian community came into play here as well. In their search for true wisdom (*sophia*: 1 Cor 1:22) some of the members of the community had embraced a naive spiritualism. They thought of themselves as the "spirituals" (*pneumatikoi*: see 2:15) who lived on a superior plane. This permitted a disdain for the physical. Bodily actions were considered indifferent because real life was in the higher realm of the mind (5:1-2). This led to the kind of overconfidence Paul is warning against. The "strong" felt they could eat meat sacrificed to idols because they knew the idols did not exist; but Paul shows them that this bodily action compromised them more than they realized. On the positive side, he emphasizes the importance of the physical sharing of the cup and the bread, and stresses that these bodily actions bring a real sharing in the body and blood of Christ.

---

[3]"Eucharist and Community in First Corinthians," *Worship* 51 (1977), 59. See also Ernst Käsemann, "The Pauline Doctrine of the Lord's Supper," in *Essays on New Testament Themes* (Studies in Biblical Theology 41; London: SCM, 1964), 128.

[4]The focus on altar and sacrifice shows that already at this early stage sacrificial terminology was being used in discussion of the Eucharist. Sacrifice as such is not the point of Paul's comparison here, however, and should not be overstressed. See Michel Gourgues, "Eucharistie et communauté chez saint Paul et les synoptiques," *Eglise et Théologie* 13 (1982) 71-73.

The Lord's Supper (1 Cor 11:17-34)

The general context here is Paul's concern with order in the Christian assemblies (see 11:6; 14:23). But more is at stake than order in the Corinthian conduct of the Lord's Supper. Paul sees a threat to the very meaning and purpose of the Eucharist. The divisions he mentioned at the beginning of the letter (1:10-13) are invading the heart of community worship. Instead of a meal of unity the Supper has become a sacrament of division.

The chiastic pattern observed in the textual setting for the "cup of blessing" passage (10:14-22) is also used by Paul here as he deals with the Corinthian observance of the Lord's Supper (11:17-34). First he describes the abuses caused by social and economic differences (vv 17-22), then he presents the example of Jesus at the Last Supper in the narrative familiar from their liturgy (vv 23-26), and finally returns to the abuses and some of the theological consequences (vv 27-34).

Recent study has shed light on the social situation which fostered the aberrations at Corinth.[5] As the Christian community grew, it became more and more difficult to find a place which could accommodate a large assembly indoors. It was natural to look to the large homes of the wealthy members of the community (1 Cor 1:11,16; Rom 16:5; Col 4:15). Archaeology has shown that the typical large home of the period could accommodate about fifty people for a meal, ten in the *triclinium* (dining room), where the guests reclined on couches, and forty in the *atrium* (courtyard), where the guests sat around a central pool. In the hospitality of the time, it was typical for the host to invite his or her closest friends and business colleagues (who were on the same social level) into the *triclinium*, where food and service were at their best, and to arrange a secondary fare for guests assigned to the *atrium*.

At the time Paul was writing, a regular meal was still connected with the Eucharist, though the Eucharist was no longer part of the meal, but followed it. Paul is horrified to find

[5]See especially Gerd Theissen, *The Social Setting of Pauline Christianity* (Philadelphia: Fortress, 1982); and Jerome Murphy-O'Connor, *St. Paul's Corinth: Texts and Archaeology* (Good News Studies 6; Wilmington: Glazier, 1983), 153-72.

that social hierarchies and prejudices have been allowed to infiltrate the central act of worship. The Corinthians have so misunderstood the Lord's Supper that Paul doubts whether what they are doing *is* the Lord's Supper. "When you come together, it is not the Lord's supper that you eat" (vv 17, 20). Each person is intent on getting the best place and the best meal, without concern for the humiliation of the poorer members (v 22).

In order to help the Corinthians re-establish the correct understanding and practice of the Eucharist, Paul recalls the action of Jesus at the Last Supper with the institution narrative familiar from their own liturgy, and then reminds them of the meaning of this Lord's Supper.[6] His narrative is very similar to that of Luke, except that the expiatory words "which is poured out for you" are omitted from the cup-word and there is a second admonition to "do this in remembrance of me" (v 25).

Paul's account situates the institution of the Eucharist in a context of betrayal, as do the Synoptic versions (Mk 14:18-21, Mt 26:21-25; Lk 22:21-23). In the Synoptics, the betrayer is mentioned before or after the institution, but in First Corinthians the betrayal is part of the narrative itself. Since Paul rarely refers to the earthly life of Jesus, this is probably part of the liturgical tradition. But mention of the betrayer at this point serves Paul as an ironic commentary on the abuses in the Corinthian Eucharist.[7]

The tradition Paul and Luke are following has atonement language with the bread-word rather than with the cup-word as in Mark/Matthew. In Paul's narrative, this is simply "which is for you" (*hyper hymōn*)" (v 24). The Mark/Matthew account is heir to a more primitive tradition in connecting the explanatory phrases with the cup-word, where it suits the character of the *Birkat Ha-Mazon*.[8] The phrase "for many" (Mk 14:24/Mt 26:28), a Semiticism, is also more primitive than

[6]There is nothing in Paul's narrative to indicate whether or not he considered the Last Supper a Passover meal. He is, however, aware of the paschal connotations of Jesus' death (1 Cor 5:7).

[7]See Mary Ann Getty, *First Corinthians, Second Corinthians* (Collegeville Bible Commentary 7; Collegeville: Liturgical Press, 1983), 54.

[8]See Chapter Three.

"for you." The "after supper" setting (v 25), however, more aptly reflects Jewish meal structure than "as they were eating" (Mk 14:22; Mt 26:26).

We have already noted that the Paul/Luke form of the cup-word represents the earlier stage of tradition: "This cup is the new covenant in my blood"(v 25). The adjective "new" emphasizes the reference to the covenant promised by Jeremiah (Jer 31:31-34), though the theme of the Sinai covenant (which is the "old covenant" reference in the mind of the prophet) is also present. Hans Conzelman has noted that in Mark/Matthew, "covenant" is a definition of "blood," while in Paul/Luke, "blood" is a definition of "covenant."[9] In this combination, the interior covenant envisaged by Jeremiah retains its connection with the covenant sacrifice of Moses. The implications of covenant might have been useful in addressing the disunity at Corinth, but Paul does not capitalize on this theme (see 2 Cor 3:6).

After the second remembrance-word, which marks the end of the received narrative, Paul adds immediately a verse which is his extension and interpretation of the admonition: "For as often as you eat this bread and drink this cup you proclaim the Lord's death until he comes" (v 26). Because of their interlocking in Paul's thought, this verse and the remembrance-saying must be held together in seeking Paul's meaning. Verse 26 is not part of the tradition Paul has received, but it represents a recapitulation of that tradition as he understood it.[10] When Paul describes the Eucharist as a proclamation of the *death* of Jesus, he is not denying its witness to the resurrection. After all, it is the *Lord's* Supper, and "Lord" is Paul's favorite title for the risen Jesus (Rom 10:9; 1 Cor 12:3; Phil 2:11). The phrase "Lord's death," in fact, contains a resurrection allusion that "Jesus' death" does not. But the situation at Corinth and the particular misunderstanding of the Eucharist there required Paul to emphasize the death.

---

[9] *1 Corinthians*, 199.

[10] Beverly Roberts Gaventa, "'You Proclaim the Lord's Death': 1 Corinthians 11:26 and Paul's Understanding of Worship," *RevExp* 80 (1983) 377-87, 378-79. Eugene LaVerdiere calls this verse a "one-line summary of Paul's eucharistic theology": "Do this in Remembrance of Me," *Emmanuel* 90 (1984), 366.

The exaggerated spiritualism already mentioned made it difficult for the Corinthians to come to grips with Jesus' crucifixion and death. They were infected with a philosophy which considered the body insignificant. For some of them (probably those Paul refers to as the Christ-faction: 1:12), Jesus was no longer to be thought of in human terms but as the Lord of Glory. The resurrection had blotted out his human history, particularly his suffering. His followers now shared in Christ's exaltation by a superior wisdom and perfection, and had no time for human weakness, theirs or others.[11]

Paul attacks this error immediately at the beginning of First Corinthians, proclaiming the "word of the cross" (1:18): "We preach Christ crucified, a stumbling block to Jews and folly to Gentiles, but to those who are called, both Jews and Greeks, Christ the power of God and the wisdom of God" (vv 22-24). The Corinthians had expected Paul to vie with other popular preachers of the time in spinning a web of high-flown philosophy, but he proclaimed the Cross. "I decided to know nothing among you except Jesus Christ and him crucified" (2:2). The death of Jesus was not just an unfortunate preliminary to his exaltation and glory, but was at the heart of his mission and message of salvation. Jesus laid down his life in love for others (8:11; see Gal 2:20); this is what his dying meant, and this is what his life meant. It was not only a saving action, but also a model, a radical demonstration of God's plan for the sharing of life among all his children. "He died for all, that those who live might live no longer for themselves but for him who for their sake died and was raised" (2 Cor 5:15). Those who disdained the suffering and death of Jesus were undermining the meaning of his saving mission and of their own Christian life.[12]

This misunderstanding had come to a head in the Corinthian celebration. Far from being the sacramental focus of their Christian community life and faith, the Lord's Supper was sacramentalizing their division and error. At the Last Supper

---

[11]Jerome Murphy-O'Connor, *1 Corinthians* (New Testament Message 10; Wilmington: Glazier, 1979), 11-22.

[12]Murphy-O'Connor, "Eucharist and Community," 61-62.

"on the night when he was betrayed" (1 Cor 11:23) Jesus had used the meal to dramatize the covenant unity of himself and his disciples and to foretell his death as a giving of his life "for you" (v 24). The celebration of the Supper in the post-resurrection community would be done "in remembrance of me" (v 25), not just an imitation of ritual actions, but a memorial of the deeper meaning of Jesus' life and death and his disciples' own life and death in union with him. There is a debate among scholars over the interpretation of the word "proclaim" in verse 26. Does "proclaim the death of the Lord" mean that Paul is envisaging a retelling of the passion or a homily explaining the meaning of the rite, or does he mean that the Supper itself is a proclamation? Surely the latter is the more natural sense of his words. Every time Christians share the Lord's Supper they proclaim the meaning of the death of the Lord and its implications in the world "until he comes." [13]

The meaning of "remembrance" (*anamnēsis*) in Jesus' admonition has also been the subject of extensive discussion. Is the Supper ritual a reminder of Jesus much as a snapshot is a memento of a loved one, or is there more? And who is the reminder for? Joachim Jeremias defended the position that the proclamation of the death of the Lord at the Supper reminds God of the unfulfilled climax of the work of redemption. The Lord's Supper is celebrated until he comes, that is, until the climax is reached. Jeremias found the basis for this interpretation in examples from the Greek Old Testament. The holocausts and burnt-offerings were meant to be "remembrance before your God" (Num 10:10). The atonement money from the census was to be a "remembrance before the Lord" (Ex 30:16). The sons of Aaron sounded their trumpets, making "a great noise to be heard for remembrance before the Most High" (Sir 50:16).[14]

This is not the most familiar sense of the call to remembrance. The ordinary interpretation is that the Lord's Supper is to be celebrated to remind us, the disciples, of what Jesus did and what it means for us. Jeremias' interpretation has not

---

[13]See the discussion in Gaventa, "You Proclaim," 380-85.
[14]Jeremias, *Eucharistic Words*, 237-55.

aroused wide support over the subsequent decades. But lately scholars have become aware that *both* ideas may be contained in the call to remember: the Eucharist as a reminder to God and as a reminder to the followers of Jesus.[15] God is reminded of his covenant promises in Jesus so that he will fulfill them, and the disciples are reminded of Jesus' self-gift in life and death so that they may imitate his example. The Eucharist looks to the past, the redemptive act of Jesus, to the present, the appropriation of the covenant by the community of his followers, and to the future, the eschatological fulfillment.

The commemoration on the part of the participants is not simply something in their subjective memory. In Hebrew thought, the thing remembered comes alive to the person as a present and effective reality. The Mishnah instructs that in the celebration of the Passover "a man must regard himself as if he came forth himself out of Egypt"(Pesahim 10:4). This seems to be the sense of Moses' words to the Israelites: "Not with our fathers did the Lord make this covenant, but with us, who are all of us here alive this day" (Dt 5:3). The past event is not transferred to the present, but a new event of the same kind occurs as the moment of redemptive time from the past initiates a genuine encounter in the present. In the Eucharist as a "memorial" of Christ, his presence and power are released anew in the assembly of his followers.[16]

The Corinthian celebration was not a true remembrance of Jesus, because they had forgotten the meaning of his life and death. They were busy with their individual pursuits of eating and social positioning. But the Supper was meant to be a memorial of Jesus' death "for you" (plural: v 24); the ritual action can carry this meaning only if the participants have the same attitude as Jesus. In Second Corinthians, Paul describes

---

[15]See David Gregg, *Anamnēsis in the Eucharist* (Grove Liturgical Study No. 5; Bramcote: Grove Books, 1976); Fritz Chenderlin, "*Do This as My Memorial*": *The Semantic and Conceptual Background and Value of Anamnēsis in* 1 *Corinthians* (An Bib 99; Rome: Biblical Institute Press, 1982).

[16]Brevard S. Childs, *Memory and Tradition in Israel* (London: SCM, 1962) 84. Nils A. Dahl even refers to a "remembering in the future" on the basis of Hebrews 11:22: "By faith Joseph, at the end of his life, remembered (*emnēmoneusen*) the exodus of the Israelites": "*Anamnēsis*: Memory and Commemoration in Early Christianity," *Jesus in the Memory of the Early Church* (Minneapolis: Augsburg, 1976), 12.

the Christian existence as "always carrying in the body the death of Jesus, so that the life of Jesus may also be manifested in our bodies" (2 Cor 4:10). To carry Jesus' death (*nekrōsis*— or better, his "dying": NAB) means to have his loving, self-emptying attitude. This is essential for receiving the "new covenant in my blood" which is accepted by each believer and sealed in the community Eucharist.[17]

After speaking of the Lord's Supper as the proclamation of the death of the Lord, Paul draws a further conclusion: "Whoever, *therefore* (*hōste*), eats the bread or drinks the cup of the Lord in an unworthy manner will be guilty of profaning the body and blood of the Lord" (11:27). The participant who joins the celebration with selfish motives is not proclaiming the death of the Lord but instead becomes one of those who caused the death. The proclaimer becomes a persecutor.[18]

The idea is repeated in verse 29: "For any one who eats and drinks without discerning the body eats and drinks judgment upon himself." Is "the body" here the same as "The body of the Lord" in verse 27, and therefore is this another admonition to distinguish the Eucharist from ordinary food? Or does "the body" here mean the community of the faithful?[19] The latter interpretation is to be preferred in the context of the Corinthian Eucharist. Paul is emphasizing both reverence for the eucharistic body and blood and what they mean, and reverence for the community as a necessary consequence. This interpretation is also urged by the composition of the letter, which in the following chapter (12:12-27) turns to a lengthy discourse on the Christian community as the body of Christ.

---

[17]The communitarian nature of the Eucharist is explored in Gourgues, Eucharistie et communauté," especially 61-66.

[18]Käsemann, "The Pauline Doctrine," 123. E. Schweizer interprets this unworthiness (in light of 8:11-12) as primarily a disregard for the poor and weak members of the community: *The Lord's Supper*, 6.

[19]The Western text adds "worthily" after "drinks" and "of the Lord" after "body" in order to bring the verse into line with verse 29. See Metzger, *A Textual Commentary*, 562-63.

Summary

Our knowledge of Paul's theology of the Eucharist and of liturgical practice in his communities comes from First Corinthians, where Paul deals with the Eucharist in addressing community problems. He is presenting the tradition that had been passed on to him in Antioch in the early 40's.

Paul's first mention of the Eucharist comes in connection with a question about the propriety of eating meat which had been left over from pagan sacrifices. One group of Corinthians had no qualms about this but another found it scandalous. Paul argues from the shared Christian conviction about what happens in the eucharistic sharing of the cup and the bread to what happens in the consuming of the meat from idol sacrifice. Paul's premise about the Eucharist is that the bread and wine is a real sharing in the body and blood of Christ (1 Cor 10:14-22).

Later Paul addresses the Corinthian conduct of the Lord's Supper directly (1 Cor 11:17-34). He is appalled that social inequities are being allowed to frustrate the unity of the celebration and its very meaning. Paul recalls to attention the words of the institution narrative in the liturgy. This version is close to that of Luke, but has a second remembrance-saying; the meaning of this remembrance as Paul understands it is added in verse 26: "You proclaim the Lord's death until he comes."

Abuses were keeping the Corinthian Eucharist from being an authentic memorial of Jesus. He had given his life in love for the salvation of the people. Their selfishness was putting them in the camp of those who had put Jesus to death. They must disown their spiritual elitism and come to grips with the dying of Jesus, his self-emptying love, in their own lives. Without this, they will remain guilty of the body and blood of the Lord (v 27), and they will be drinking judgment, not salvation, by failing to discern the true nature of the community as the body of Christ (v 29). Paul urges a deeper awareness of the meaning of the new covenant shared in the Lord's Supper, and thus an authentic proclamation of the Lord's death until he comes in glory.

6

The Eucharist of Mark

First Corinthians' explicit and detailed discussion of the Eucharist drops into early Christian literature as into a sea of silence. It is the first datable reference we have, and fifteen years will pass before another of our documents will address the issue. We know from the New Testament writings which deal with the Eucharist that much development was underway both before and after the letter of Paul. Most of this was unwritten experience, but there was also a written tradition, especially in the area of community worship. All of this information is scattered, however, and its reconstruction is debatable. How significant it is, then, that when the next explicit and datable treatment appears around 70, a treatment with obvious differences from that of Paul, it bears witness to a core of common eucharistic faith and practice. The Gospel of Mark addresses the question of the Eucharist in a different context and from a different point of view, but his presentation enriches rather than contradicts the Pauline approach.

During the years following Paul's ministry to Corinth, the Church continued to spread throughout the Roman Empire and to develop internally. The period is marked by a growing awareness of the delay of the parousia. In earlier years, the disciples had lived in expectancy of an immediate return of the Lord (1 Thess 1:10; 4:15), but by the mid-50's this was changing. Christians were becoming more and more aware that the time of the Church might be a long period, and that many of them would die before the end. This conviction was only confirmed by the death in the 60's of the great leaders,

Peter, Paul, and James, and others. Out of this realization arose the need for a written record of the life and teaching of Jesus. If the witnesses die, how will we remember? Mark's Gospel is designed to record the mission and message of Jesus, but at the same time to interpret its meaning in light of current developments in his Church. How does the life, the teaching, the victory of Jesus relate to what is happening in our lives now?

It is in this context that the Eucharist is treated in the Gospel of Mark. Like Paul (but less noticeably), Mark is dealing with some contemporary abuses while presenting the meaning of the Eucharist. But Mark is also intent on showing the origin of the Eucharist in the ministry of Jesus and the meaning of the Last Supper in its own setting. Paul introduces the issue because of his contemporary situation and parenthetically refers to the institution of the Eucharist; Mark, on the other hand, is presenting the origin of the Eucharist in the time of Jesus and parenthetically referring to the local scene.

We can detect the eucharistic theology of Mark primarily in three places in his narrative: in the stories of the multiplication of the loaves, in passages which develop the theme of the cup, and in the framing and editing of the Supper account.

The Feeding Stories (6:32-44; 8:1-10)

The feeding of the five thousand with five loaves and two fish is one of the few stories contained in all four of the Gospels (Mk 6:32-44; Mt 14:13-21; Lk 9:10-17; Jn 6:1-15). In addition to this, Mark and Matthew have a second story of the feeding of four thousand with seven loaves and a few fish. The general view today is that the second story is a doublet of the first rather than a report of a different incident.[1] The first feeding takes place in Jewish territory, the second in the Decapolis

---

[1]The discussion is summarized in standard works like Vincent Taylor, *The Gospel According to St. Mark* (London: Macmillan, 1963) 321-22; 356-57; Eduard Schweizer, *The Good News According to Mark* (Richmond: John Knox, 1970), 136-38.

beyond the Sea of Galilee, Gentile territory. This is the key to Mark's use of the stories.

These stories from Jesus' ministry were already connected with the Eucharist by the Christian community before they came to the evangelists. Preachers had made the connection clear by using words familiar from the institution narrative to describe Jesus' actions in the feeding of the crowds. In the account of the first feeding, Jesus took the loaves and fish, looked up to heaven, [2]blessed (*eulogēsen*), broke the bread and gave it to the disciples (Mk 6:41; Mt 14:19; Lk 9:16). In the account of the second feeding, the words are "took," "gave thanks" (*eucharistēsas*), "broke," and "gave" (Mk 8:6; Mt 15:35). Mark's emphasis on the lateness of the hour (6:35) may intimate a parallel with the Last Supper.[3] The instructions to "recline" and to "lie down," unnatural for a desert place, are understandable in connection with the Last Supper[3] (See *anapesein* in 8:6 and Lk 22:14). In the second story, the focus is not on food as such, but on bread. In both stories, the fragments are described as *klasmata*, a term for the Eucharist in the Didache (IX: 3-4).

The feeding stories recall two important antecedents in Israelite history: a multiplication of loaves and grain by the prophet Elisha during a time of famine (2 Kings 4:42-44), and the feeding of the people by the miraculous manna in the wilderness (Ex 16:13-35). The implication is that Jesus possesses the power and authority of the ancient prophets. In the Elisha story, one hundred men were fed from twenty barley loaves and a few ears of grain; they ate, and there was some left over. The telling of the story of Jesus' multiplication of bread and fish has probably been affected by details from this passage, such as the specification of barley loaves by John (Jn 6:9) and the mention of leftovers in all the accounts (which, however, have given meaning to this detail by the use of symbolic numbers).

---

[2]The account of the multiplication of the loaves in Mark is so obviously eucharistic that the words "looking up to heaven" became part of the consecration formula in the Roman Canon (Eucharistic Prayer I).

[3]Sanae Masuda, "The Good News of the Miracle of the Bread: The Tradition and its Markan Redaction," *NTS* 28 (1982), 192.

The connection of the feeding stories with the Exodus theme of bread in the wilderness is also by allusion rather than by direct application. The bread and fish echo the manna and quail (flesh from the sea) of the wilderness; and the "green grass" of the desert (Mk 6:39) insinuates the eschatological change of the wilderness into a land of fertility and rest.[4] The neat arrangement "in groups" (v 40) may be a reminder of the host of Israel in their encampments.[5] The collection of the fragments reflects messianic abundance and also shows, that, unlike the manna which could not be held over till the next day, the bread that Jesus gives does not decay.[6]

In the Exodus account, the gift of manna and quail is a response to the murmuring of the people, who imply that Moses (and by implication God) has led them into the desert not to rescue them from slavery in Egypt but to kill them. In the Gospel, the initiative comes rather from the compassion of Jesus who, aware of the people's need, gives them food for spirit and body, his teaching and the bread and fish.

There is a contrast between the reaction of the disciples and of Jesus. When the disciples notice the people's need, they tell Jesus to "send them away"; but Jesus says "You give them something to eat" (vv 36-37), encouraging them to take responsibility, as he has, for providing for them.[7] Through Jesus' compassion, the disciples are now given a means of serving the needs of the people; later he will provide the leaders of the Christian community with a more substantial means of feeding the people.

The words Mark uses to describe the crowds, "like sheep without a shepherd," recall another Moses passage in which the prophet asks the Lord for a successor "that the congregation of the Lord may not be as sheep which have no shepherd" (Num 27:17). Jesus fulfills the role of this new leader of the

---

[4] Lamar Williamson, Jr., "An Exposition of Mark 6:30-44," *Int* 30 (1976) 172-73.

[5] The NAB translates *prasiai prasiai* as "neatly arranged like flower beds."

[6] The manna theme is underscored by John (Jn 6:27); another wilderness allusion in the Fourth Gospel is the murmuring by the Jews (6:41; using the word *gogguzo* as in Ex 16: 7-8 LXX).

[7] William Barclay, *The Gospel of Mark* (Daily Study Bible; Philadelphia: Westminster, 1975), 158.

people in a superior way and his compassion feeds them in a superior way by the eucharistic food which is foreshadowed by the bread and fish.

The second feeding has subtle changes which indicate a mission to the Gentiles (that is, a universal mission to the whole world). Four thousand are fed, four being a number symbolic of the four corners of the earth (Rev 7:1). This time, some of the people have "come a long way" (8:3), a probable allusion to the presence in the early Church of Greeks from all over the Empire. The twelve baskets of the first feeding are an obvious reference to the tribes of Israel, but seven is a number symbolic of universalism; there are seven loaves and seven baskets. Even the words for basket in the two narratives are indicative: *kophinos* (6:43) was a wicker basket in which Jews carried food; *spyris* (8:8) was a container for much larger quantities and might be large enough to hold a man. The use of *eulogēsas* (blessed) with fish as the object rather than God (8:7) is a sign of Hellenistic rather than Hebrew mentality.

The combination of the two stories responded to the question which agonized the early Church: should the Church make baptism and Church membership available to non-Jews? And if so, should there be any restrictions or special rules for Gentiles? This debate is reflected in Paul's letters, especially Galatians, and in the Acts of the Apostles. There were various positions along the spectrum of early Christian thought.[8] Mark uses the stories of the multiplication of loaves and fish to show that Jesus' mission is all-inclusive. The Eucharist is the one bread for all the different peoples.[9] The implication of 8:3 may be that if the "foreigners" are deprived of this eucharistic bread they will "faint on the way."

The theme of the one loaf is continued in the later discussion in the boat. Mark introduces this episode with the strange statement: "Now they had forgotten to bring bread; and they had only one loaf with them in the boat" (8:14). Matthew has avoided the contradiction by making no mention of the one

[8]This is one of the themes addressed in R.E. Brown, *The Churches the Apostles Left Behind* (New York: Paulist, 1984).

[9]Donald Senior, "The Eucharist in Mark: Mission, Reconcilation, Hope," *BTB* 12 (1982), 69.

loaf (Mt 16:5), but in doing so has missed the point of Mark's statement. The boat is the Church and the one loaf is the one bread, Jesus himself, needed by Jew and Gentile alike. There must be no exclusion from the common eucharistic table. The one eucharistic bread binds all into one.[10] This was a hard saying for some Jewish converts. The questions of Jesus are meant to drive home the realization.

> "Do you not remember? When I broke the five loaves for the five thousand, how many baskets full of broken pieces did you take up?" They said to him, "Twelve." "And the seven for the four thousand, how many baskets full of broken pieces did you take up?" And they said to him, "Seven." And he said to them, "Do you not yet understand?" (8:18-21)

They had not understood "about the loaves" in the first feeding, either (6:52). There the lack of understanding was mentioned in connection with the walking on the water and the stilling of the storm, which should have convinced them of Jesus' power and his saving presence in their midst. The first feeding had been a clear sign of Jesus' continuing concern and care for his Hebrew brothers and sisters. They did not perceive his meaning then, and now they are closed to the meaning of the second feeding, that this concern and care extends to the Gentiles, too. They will not be able to understand the full meaning of the Eucharist shared in their communities, in which Jesus is present with all his compassion and saving grace, until they probe the meaning of Jesus' universal mission.

The Cup (10:35-45; 14:32-36)

If the bread of the Eucharist is foreshadowed in the feeding stories, the meaning of the eucharistic cup is illumined in other

---

[10]Wilfrid Harrington, *Mark* (New Testament Message 4; Wilmington: Glazier, 1979) 113. See also the excellent study of this passage by Norman A. Beck, "Reclaiming a Biblical Text: The Mark 8:14-21 Discussion about Bread in the Boat," *CBQ* 43 (1981) 49-56.

passages outside the Supper account. Just after Jesus and his disciples had made the fateful turn up the road to Jerusalem, James and John came to Jesus with the request, "Grant us to sit, one at your right hand and one at your left, in your glory" (10:37). Instead of responding directly to this question, Jesus countered with his own question, "Are you able to drink the cup that I drink, or to be baptized with the baptism with which I am baptized?" They responded glibly, "We are able." Having established its true context, Jesus returns to their request: "The cup that I drink you will drink; and with the baptism with which I am baptized, you will be baptized; but to sit at my right hand or at my left is not mine to grant, but it is for those for whom it has been prepared" (vv 38-40).

This episode comes at a climactic point in Jesus' preparation of his disciples. Immediately after Peter had identified him as the Messiah (8:29), Jesus began to reveal the suffering and death his mission would entail. Peter would not hear of it and had to be corrected. Then Jesus went further and explained the implications of his Messiahship for his disciples (vv 34-38). But when he returned to the theme a second time there was no more appreciation than before. In fact, the disciples' lack of understanding is illustrated by their quarreling about their own importance (9:30-34). The third announcement of the passion (10:33-34) immediately precedes the present passage. The obtuseness of James and John is even more apparent after this third teaching. Jesus' counterquestion is meant to draw them back to the true implications of following him as disciples: Can you drink the cup? Drinking the cup and being baptized with his baptism means sharing his redemptive suffering and being willing to follow him to death. In this passage the true implications of Eucharist (and Baptism) come into focus.[11]

The cup appears in a symbolic way after the Supper as well, when Jesus goes with his disciples to the garden of Gethsemane. Even Jesus, who had invited his followers to drink the cup of suffering with him, recoils before the ultimate challenge. He is "greatly distressed and troubled" and prays: "Abba, Father, all

[11]See the examination of the theological and spiritual issues by Eugene LaVerdiere, "Can You Drink the Cup?" *Emmanuel* 89 (1983) 490-95.

things are possible to thee; remove this cup from me: yet not what I will but what thou wilt" (14:33-36). Contemporary and later disciples learn from Jesus' example that even with a commitment to drink the cup, there is need for the support of the community (which may fail as in the case of the disciples in the garden), but above all of prayer to the Father.

The Supper (14:22-25)

The lack of perception by the disciples noted in the episode of the boat and in connection with the predictions of suffering and death are ingredients of a general theme in Mark. The disciples' lack of comprehension is practically unrelieved throughout the Gospel. It will even be heightened in the Passion narrative with betrayal by Judas, denial by Peter, and flight by the rest of the Twelve. It comes as no surprise that this theme is present in the Supper account.[12]

The Supper is set in a tension of solidarity and betrayal. When preparing for the meal, the disciples ask, "Where will you have us go and prepare *for you* to eat the passover?" Jesus instructs them to ask, "Where is my guest room, where I am to eat the passover *with my disciples?*" (14:12-14) emphasizing the bond between them. Though two of the group are already present at the supper room, Mark says that he "came with the twelve" (v 17). They are a unity. To highlight the breach of bond to come, Judas, who is already well known to the reader (3:19), is specifically identified at this late juncture as "one of the twelve," and not only that, but as "one who is dipping bread into the dish with me," sharing an intimate moment (v 20). The narrative of the institution of the Eucharist comes immediately after this scene and Jesus' comment on the heinousness of the betrayal, and just before the prediction that all will fall away and that Peter will deny him.

The words and actions of Jesus are all the more striking in this setting. He does not withdraw or in any way temper his

---

[12]The themes of the Marcan Supper account are unfolded by Donald Senior, *The Passion of Jesus in the Gospel of Mark* (The Passion Series 2; Wilmington: Glazier, 1984) 52-62.

invitation to the disciples to intimate friendship and a share in his mission. The significant words, "took . . . blessed . . . broke . . . gave," remind us that this is the third in a series of feeding stories. Earlier he had given bread to the disciples for their own sustenance and "to set before the people" (6:41; 8:60). Now he shares with them his own body and blood, himself. This too they will set before the people. Mark points out that when the cup was offered, "they all drank of it" (14:23). When James and John had agreed to drink the cup (10:39), Jesus knew what they were saying but they did not. By the time Mark's Gospel was written, James' martyrdom was an event of Christian history (Acts 12:2). The cup Jesus offers to all his disciples is a share in his messianic suffering. Everyone who follows Jesus must be willing to drink the cup. But now we know that the eucharistic cup is also an offer of intimate union with Jesus: it contains "my blood of the covenant, poured out for many" —Jesus giving himself to them and for them as the Servant who offers his life "as a ransom for many" (10:45).

The phrase "blood of the covenant" is a direct allusion to the Sinai covenant, when Moses splashed the blood of the offerings on the altar and on the people (Ex 24:5-8). The bond between God and his people was ratified in the sacrificial animal's blood, symbolizing a sharing of life (Dt 12:23). The animal was neither divine nor human, but now the covenant is ratified in the blood of Jesus, son of God and son of man. Just as at Sinai the people were first asked to agree to the demands of the relationship (Ex 24:3), so at the Last Supper the disciples are asked to drink from the cup as a sign of their willingness to share the destiny of Jesus.

They are now united in covenant with Jesus and, in spite of their fears, have accepted the vocation of sharing his mission and all that it entails. In the midst of mention of betrayal and suffering there is a mood of triumph and hope, however. Jesus looks beyond his death and the failure of his followers to the accomplishment of the kingdom (v 24) and promises a reconciliation in spite of the betrayal (v 28). In Mark's community this would have sent a message of forgiveness and acceptance to members of the community who had fallen away in times of persecution (4:16-17). It would also be a call to reconciliation among divided Christians, leading to covenant renewal in the Eucharist. The Marcan Eucharist is a scene of unity, openness, and reconciliation.

Summary

During the decade and a half between the time of First Corinthians and the writing of the Gospel of Mark, the Christian community was celebrating the Eucharist in various localities and social contexts and with different theological emphases. Mark describes a Eucharist with differences in theological theme and variations in the institution narrative compared to Paul. But a common core of eucharistic faith and practice is evident.

Mark situates the account of the institution of the Eucharist in a context of failure and betrayal. This serves to highlight the theme of reconciliation present in Jesus' offer of himself to his disciples during the Last Supper. He does not withhold himself from them and even promises a reunion after the dread events to come. This theme of openness as a eucharistic motif had been developed earlier in the two stories of the feeding in the desert. The Jews and Gentiles are both fed by Jesus, who is the one loaf for everyone. Mark's Church could read in this an admonition to reconcile after quarrels or divisions and to remain open to sharing the Eucharist with converts of different national and religious backgrounds.

The cup at the Last Supper has a literal function in containing Jesus' blood of the covenant. But symbolically it means the redemptive suffering of Jesus. The disciples' drinking of the cup gives them solidarity in Jesus' covenant, but it also implies a commitment to his servant ministry and to the suffering and death it may entail. His life is being poured out in sacrifice; this is the model for their discipleship.

7

The Eucharist of Matthew

Matthew's indebtedness to the Gospel of Mark has already been noted in reference to the narratives of eucharistic institution, where the tradition shared by Mark and Matthew is distinguished from that of Paul and Luke. Matthew also follows Mark in the other passages we have used to discern Mark's eucharistic theology: the feeding stories and the statements about the cup in response to Zebedee's sons' request and in the agony in the Garden. At first glance it might seem that Matthew is simply repeating the eucharistic teaching of Mark. The theme of the cup, for example, is certainly unchanged. But Matthew does reveal a distinctive vision of the Eucharist within the themes of his Gospel. This is brought to the fore by some changes of emphasis in the presentation of the feeding stories and the Last Supper narrative. Besides this, everything in Matthew's Gospel is affected by the quite different context in which he is addressing his community.

Most scholars today place the writing of Matthew's Gospel in the mid-80's (at roughly the same time as the writings of Luke). Mark had written probably from Rome just at the time the Jewish nation was facing the profound crisis of the crushing of the Zealot rebellion and the destruction of the temple. By Matthew's time, the form of Judaism had changed dramatically. No longer did Jewish life center around Jerusalem and the temple liturgy. Jewish religious life now focused on the scattered synagogues where the new leaders, the Pharisees, were doing all they could to strengthen the weakened Jewish community. Their insistence on strict uniformity in Jewish thought and practice raised problems for Jewish Christians which had not existed in the tolerant days before 70 A.D. They were being forcibly separated from their ancient heritage and sometimes experienced even the acute pain of family division.

Matthew was probably writing in Syria to a Church with a strong Jewish identity. More and more Gentiles were coming into the community, people with little appreciation for Jewish traditions. The Jewish Christians felt their roots being undercut and wondered about the future direction of a mixed community. Matthew wrote in this context of uncertainty, alienation, and loss. As we examine the passages which shed light on Matthew's eucharistic theology, this context will be kept in mind.

The Feeding Stories (Mt 14:13-21; 15:21-28)

The discussion of the feeding stories in Mark is presupposed in our examination of accounts in Matthew. Here, too, the thematic background is the Sinai desert of the Exodus wandering (14:13; 15:4). But the second multiplication does not take place in Gentile territory. There is no indication that Matthew understands the double feeding as an expression of Jesus' universal mission, though that meaning would have served his purpose as appropriately as it did Mark's.[1] Perhaps in conjunction with the Scripture fulfillment motif of his Gospel (e.g. 1:22-23; 8:17; 13:34-35), Matthew understands the feeding in the desert as a sign of messianic fulfillment, but if so, he has done nothing to make this specific. The eucharistic theme is present, however, and, if anything, is heightened in Matthew. His abbreviations of Mark highlight the cultic tone, for example, in the omissions of the mention of the fish in the distribution and collection of the first feeding (14:19-20; Mk 6:41-43), and at the separate blessing of the fish in the second (15:36; Mk 8:7).

---

[1] Matthew uses the two feeding stories as a doublet, a technique of which he is fond: see 9:27-31/20:29-34 (blind men); 9:32-34/12:22-24 (dumb man); 12:38-42/16:1-4 (request for a sign).

The Eucharist of Matthew   95

Even though Matthew does not follow Mark in differen-
tiating the two feedings as ministries to Jews and Gentiles, he
does present these events as expressions of the thrust of Jesus'
messianic mission. Two stresses are noteworthy in this regard.
The first is Matthew's editorial changes which set the stories in
the context of healing. The mention of the compassion of Jesus
in Mark's account (Mk 6:34; 8:2; Mt 14:14; 15:32) fits hand in
glove with a favorite Matthean theme. To the mention of
Jesus' compassion on the crowd before the first feeding
Matthew adds the comment, " . . . and he healed their sick"
(14:14). In an earlier passage, unique to Matthew, the
evangelist had summarized the ministry of Jesus as teaching,
preaching and healing. The compassion of Jesus was
emphasized, using the same word (*splangchnizomai*) and the
same image (sheep without a shepherd) used by Mark in the
feeding stories.

> And Jesus went about all the cities and villages, teaching in
> their synagogues and preaching the gospel of the kingdom,
> and healing every disease and every infirmity. When he saw
> the crowd, he had compassion for them, because they were
> harassed and helpless, like sheep without a shepherd (Mt
> 9:35-36).

Matthew seems to have seized on the image of the "sheep
without a shepherd" as an apt description of the community to
which he was ministering by his writing. By transferring the
image to an earlier stage of the gospel story, he makes this the
keynote for the sending out of the twelve apostles (10:1-5). The
upheaval in Judaism had left angry scars in Matthew's
community. Close relationships were ruptured by betrayal and
hatred. Jesus' missionary instructions to the Twelve refer to
these divisions in words placed much later in the Gospels of
Mark and Luke:

> Brother will deliver up brother to death, and the father his
> child, and children will rise against parents and have them
> put to death, and you will be hated by all for my sake
> (10:21-22; Mk 13:12-13; Lk 21:16-17).

Jesus' compassion is expressed throughout the Gospel in his mercy, forgiveness and healing, and these qualities are necessary also in his true disciples. This is a vital theme of the Sermon on the Mount (Mt 5-7). The beatitudes speak of the sorrowing and the persecuted and slandered, of which there were many in Matthew's community, but also of the merciful and the peacemakers (5:1-12).[2] The disciples are admonished against anger and abusive language (5:22) and are told to give no resistance to injury (v 39). They are to love their enemies and pray for their persecutors (vv 44). The only restriction Jesus put on prayer is found in the instruction to "leave your gift before the altar" until there is reconciliation with your brother (v 24; see Mk 11:25).[3]

In their prayer, Christians are to look to the Father for forgiveness (6:12). Jesus expresses the forgiving will of God in calling sinners (9:13). The gift of forgiveness is a call to forgive and be merciful. The disciple's prayer is "forgive us our debts, as we also have forgiven our debtors" (6:12), which is followed by the warning "If you do not forgive, neither will your Father forgive you" (v 15). The same warning appears at the end of the parable of the merciless steward (18:35).[4]

Some changes Matthew has made in the two passages leading up to the account of the second feeding are understandable in the light of his mercy theme. In the story of the Canaanite woman asking help for her sick daughter, Matthew adds the plea "Have mercy (*eleēson*) on me" (15:22; Mk 7:25), and at the conclusion makes it clear that she was "healed instantly." Immediately preceding the feeding of the four thousand, Mark tells the story of the healing of the deaf-mute in the Decapolis (Mk 7:31-37). In place of this, Matthew

---

[2] *Eleeō* (have mercy) is more frequent in Matthew than in the other Gospels; *eirēnopoioi* (peacemakers) is used in the New Testament only at Mt 5:9.

[3] In its original context, this saying referred to Jerusalem temple worship. By the time of Matthew's use of it, there was no Jewish altar or temple; in its new context the saying refers to Christian ritual worship, including the Eucharist.

[4] See Leonard Doohan, *Matthew: Spirituality for the 80's and 90's* (Santa Fe: Bear, 1985), 110-111. Donald Senior, *The Passion of Jesus in the Gospel of Matthew* (The Passion Series 1; Wilmington: Glazier, 1985), 69, notes: "Reconciliation and forgiveness become the hallmark of the Matthean Jesus."

describes a general mission to "the lame, the maimed, the blind, the dumb, and many others." They laid them at his feet, "and he healed them" (Mk 15:29-31). The feeding in the desert is part of this compassionate healing ministry. In Matthew's theology, the eucharistic feeding is also not only nourishing but in a special way healing. At the Last Supper this will center on the "inner healing" of forgiveness (26:28).

The second stress besides healing is the messianic abundance of the multiplication of loaves in the desert. In both stories, Matthew has expanded the number of people served to include women and children in addition to the five thousand and the four thousand men (14:44; 15:38). Is this a reference to some eucharistic discrimination in the communities for whom Matthew is writing? It is not unthinkable, because the male exclusivity of Jewish worship may have lingered among groups of Hebrew converts and affected liturgical practice among the Christians to whom Matthew was writing. This embellishment, for whatever reason, serves to underscore the universalism already noted in Mark's account.

As in Mark, in Matthew the statement "They all ate and were satisified" (14:20) is a reference to the Old Testament promise of messianic fullness (Ps 132:15; Is 49:10). The collecting of the fragments makes the same point in prophetic symbol (v 21). In Matthew's Gospel this eschatological emphasis recalls the vision of the banquet in the kingdom of heaven where Gentiles will sit together with Abraham, Isaac, and Jacob (8:11). The messianic banquet theme appears in the Last Supper accounts of all three Synoptics (26:29; Mk 14:25; Lk 22:16-18).

The Last Supper (26:17-29)

Matthew follows Mark closely in the Supper narrative. The themes present in the earlier tradition and in Mark's theology are generally taken over. Differences between the two accounts are sometimes simply a reinforcement of themes already present in the received tradition. Two such distinctive stresses are signalled in the preparation scene (26:17-19): obedience as a *sine qua non* of Christian discipleship and the forgiveness of sins through the death and resurrection of Jesus.[5]

In Mark's Gospel, the disciples characteristically misunderstand (Mk 6:52; 8:21). In Matthew, on the contrary, the disciples (now identified with the Twelve: 10:1-2) understand both Jesus' teaching and who he is. They do not need instruction about the meaning of the parables (13:18, 34; Mk 4:13, 34); in the boat, they worship him as the Son of God (14:33; Mk 6:51-52). The disciples always address Jesus as "Lord"(kyrios), a post-Easter title describing his true identity (8:25; 17:4; 20:33). Only Judas addresses him as Rabbi (26:25,49). The true disciple not only calls Jesus by the appropriate name but recognizes his authority and obeys him. Jesus is teacher and master, his disciples are servants (10:24-25). They follow and obey when he commands, or as at the Supper, they go when they are sent (see 8:8-9). He makes the plans for his Passover meal and they carry them out. Later he will tell the women where the disciples are to meet him, and they obey as directed (28:10,16).[6]

In the preparation scene, not just two but all the disciples go in obedience to Jesus' command. The householder is not questioned about the place of the meal, but is simply told, "I will keep the passover at your house with my disciples"(v 18). The theme of Jesus' foreknowledge is uppermost in Mark: "They found it as he had told them" (Mk 14:16). Foreknowledge is still evident in Matthew's account in Jesus' statement, "My time is at hand" (v 18), and later in the foretelling of the betrayal, flight, and denial of the disciples, but here the voice of Jesus' authority seems to dominate.[7]

---

[5]R.H. Gundry, Matthew: A Commentary on his Literary and Theological Art (Grand Rapids, Eerdmans, 1982) 524-28, makes much of this obedience theme culminating in the double commands "Eat . . . drink" of the institution. He points out the subtle change of focus from the Passover meal to the person of Jesus in the modification of Mark's wording "that you may eat the passover" (Mk 14:12) to "prepare for you, to eat the passover" (etoimasōmen soi: Mt 26:17).

[6]Jack Dean Kingsbury, Matthew (Proclamation Commentaries; Philadelphia: Fortress, 1977), 79.

[7]Donald Senior, The Passion of Jesus 59-60, notes that this is the same sense of authority which flowed through the scenes of the entry into Jerusalem and the cleansing of the temple (Mt 21:1-13). Jesus' actions at that time brought a challenge from the temple authorities (vv 23-27).

The mention of Jesus' name in verse 17 (where Mark has a pronoun: Mk 14:12) is hardly noticeable, but it is part of the forgiveness theme in Matthew. At the beginning of his Gospel, Matthew interpreted the name of the Savior: "You shall call his name Jesus, for he will save his people from their sins" (1:21). The popular etymology of the Aramaic *Yeshua* is "Yahweh is salvation." Matthew shows his predilection for the name of Jesus throughout the Gospel, using it 154 times to 80 in Mark, and often substituting it for the pronoun, as he does twice in the preparation account and once in the institution narrative (26:17, 19, 26), and frequently throughout the passion account.[8]

The context of betrayal in which Mark presented the Last Supper is preserved in Matthew, and is even heightened to make eucharistic forgiveness more striking. The prediction of Judas' betrayal is formed into a crescendo, culminating in the dialogue between the betrayer and Jesus. The additional "Is it I?" probes the conscience of the Christian regularly celebrating the Eucharist in Matthew's Church. The contrast of the faithful and unfaithful disciples is brought out again in the titles of Jesus, "Lord" and "Rabbi." The title Lord here emphasizes acceptance of the divine authority of Jesus; but Rabbi, an unpopular term in Matthew's Church because of hostility with the synagogue, implies an allegiance on this-worldly terms.

The institution narrative follows Mark in the very inexact references to the outline of the meal and in bringing the bread and cup together. The repetition of the word "disciples" (v 26) and the addition of the command "Eat" are part of the theme of authority and obedience. The bread and cup actions are brought into closer parallel with the "Drink" command; and this also makes it possible for Jesus to interpret the cup before it is drunk. In light of the theme of the cup of suffering (taken over without change from Mark) this challenge to "all of you" provides an opportunity for decision before drinking. Do you want to drink the cup with me?

[8]Donald Senior, *The Passion Narrative According to Matthew: A Redactional Study* (BETL 39; Leuven: Leuven University Press, 1976) 25-26.

The Matthean form of the cup-word has an important addition: "This is my blood of the covenant, poured out for many *for the forgiveness of sins"*(26:28). The addition draws out implications already present in the Marcan version, but it is also the climactic statement of Matthew's theme of healing and reconciliation. The troubled sheep of Matthew's divided community are not without a shepherd. Through his death Jesus has won the ultimate healing, forgiveness of sins, and this gift is offered to his followers in the Eucharist as the solid basis for the peace and reconciliation they are seeking.[9]

The source of the phrase "blood of the covenant" in the story of Moses and the people at Sinai (Ex 24:8) has been discussed earlier. A further overtone of meaning is possible in Matthew. The phrase "blood of my covenant with you"(RSV or "blood of your covenant with me"(NAB)[10] appears in the prophecy of Zechariah (9:11) in the context of redemption. Since Matthew (uniquely among the evangelists) quotes the neighboring verse 9:9 when interpreting Jesus' entry into Jerusalem (Mt 21:5), he may also intend an allusion to Zechariah here as well. The whole passage from Zechariah reads:

Rejoice greatly, O daughter of Zion!
Shout aloud, O daughter of Jerusalem!
Lo, your king comes to you; triumphant and victorious is he,
humble and riding on an ass, on a colt the foal of an ass.
I will cut off the chariot from Ephraim and the war horse from Jerusalem;
and the battle bow shall be cut off, and he shall command peace to the nations;
his dominion shall be from sea to sea,
and from the River to the ends of the earth.

[9]Whether the Matthean addition in 26:28 is due to the Evangelist himself or comes from his community's liturgy is disputed. For the former position, see Senior, *The Passion Narrative*, 76-77; for the latter, John Meier, *The Vision of Matthew: Christ, Church and Morality in the First Gospel* (Theological Inquiries; New York: Paulist, 1979), 183.

[10]The Hebrew has "blood of your covenant."

As for you also, because of the blood of my covenant with you,
I will set your captives free from the waterless pit. (Zech 9:9-11)

The messianic king envisioned by the prophet is humble and comes with peaceful intentions. Remembering the ancient covenant of God with his people, he will give the people peace and set them free from bondage. Perhaps Matthew, who has read the Hebrew Scriptures very carefully to detect foreshadowings of Christ, finds a parallel in the progression of Zechariah's thought here and in the events of Holy Week. The death of Jesus, predicted and interpreted in the cup-word at the Last Supper, brings to climax and completion the redemptive intentions that animated Jesus as he entered Jerusalem.

The phrase "poured out for many" (v 28) recalls the ransom-saying of 20:28; both are understood as references to the Servant passage in Isaiah 52-53. Matthew has further indicated this reference by changing *hyper* (for) to *peri*, the preposition used in the Septuagint version of Isaiah 53:4: "He suffers for (*peri*) us." This change subtly brings into greater relief the idea of Jesus' death as an expiatory sacrifice.[11] Though the Mark/Matthew tradition does not speak of the *new* covenant as in the Paul/Luke tradition of the cup-word (1 Cor 11:25; Lk 22:20),[12] all these Matthean additions are consonant with the conclusion of the new covenant prophecy in Jeremiah: "I will forgive their iniquity, and I will remember their sin no more" (Jer 31:34).

The deep healing of forgiveness is available to the disciples in the Eucharist. Though Matthew makes much of obedience in the preparation for and participation in the Supper, he does not base forgiveness on obedience or faithful discipleship. Forgiveness comes through the sacrifice of Jesus, the pouring

---

[11]This use of *peri* reflects sacrificial terminology in the Septuagint: Gundry, *Matthew*, 528.

[12]A number of manuscripts from the fifth century on do have "new (*kainēs*) covenant" at Matthew 26:28, but this is presumed to have been transferred from the Lucan text.

out of his blood. It is available for "the many," that is, for all
who will have it, including the betrayer who is dipping his hand
into the dish with Jesus (v 23). Earlier, when describing the
ministry of John the Baptist, Matthew had taken care to
reserve the power of forgiving sins to Jesus alone. He omitted
the statement of Mark that John was "preaching a baptism of
repentance for the forgiveness of sins," and recorded simply
the prophet's challenge, "Repent, for the kingdom of heaven is
at hand" (3:2; Mk 1:4). The forgiveness of sins is a messianic
gift from Jesus, the fulfillment of ancient hopes. This fulfillment
is symbolized by the opening of tombs at the death of Jesus, as
the saints of old recognize the salvation they have awaited
(27:52-53).

The eschatological saying in Mk 14:25 has been taken over
by Matthew with small but significant embellishments.
Matthew uses the phrase *ap arti* (from now on) in place of
Mark's *ouketi* (no more): "I shall not drink *from now on* of this
fruit of the vine until the day when I drink it new with you in
my Father's kingdom" (v 29). In Matthew, this expression is
used to look forward to the time of the Church after the death
and resurrection of Jesus (see 23:39), and here is probably
meant to indicate the eucharistic banquet which is being eaten
regularly in the Church to which he writes. The addition of
"with you" is an emphasis in the same direction.

These last editorial refinements of the institution narrative
also reinforce the Emmanuel (God-with-us) theme of Matthew.
At the beginning of the Gospel, the conception of Jesus was
heralded as the fulfillment of the prophecy of Isaiah: "Behold,
a virgin shall conceive and bear a son, and his name shall be
called Emmanuel" (1:23; Is 7:14). Jesus will be a sign that God
is present in the midst of his people. This promise is echoed and
renewed for the future in the final words of the Gospel: "I am
with you always, to the close of the age" (28:20). These two
verses serve as a frame for the entire Gospel. The death of Jesus
has not separated him from his disciples; he is still with them.
Matthew alone reports the promise of Jesus: "Where two or
three are gathered in my name, there am I in the midst of them"
(18:20). The minor changes in the eschatological saying at the
Last Supper bring this theme to the Eucharist, where Christians
share the redeeming and forgiving presence of Jesus. The

covenant is renewed and embodied in Jesus himself, who becomes the living blood bond between God and God's people.[13]

Summary

To some extent, Matthew repeats the eucharistic theology of the Gospel of Mark, on which he is dependent. This is true, for example, of the theme of the cup of suffering. But Matthew has a particular eucharistic vision which comes through in his special themes and in his modification of the feeding stories and the Last Supper narrative. His understanding of the place of the Eucharist in Christian life is also affected by the alienation and uncertainties in his own community.

The reconciliation of weak disciples, a theme noted in Mark's presentation, remains in the Gospel of Matthew, but personal healing and forgiveness for later followers of Jesus is an important precision of this theme. The feeding stories have more of this context of healing, but omit the emphasis on the feeding of Jew and Gentile with the one bread. The forgiveness theme finds its climax in the addition "for the forgiveness of sins" in the cup-word at the Last Supper.

Matthew has edited the narrative of the Supper, beginning with the preparation, to show the role of obedience in Christian discipleship. Jesus commands and those who are true to him obey. The faithful disciples reveal their understanding of Jesus' identity by calling him "Lord," rather than "Rabbi" or "Master." Even the eating and drinking of the sacramental bread and wine is done in response to the Lord's command. "Drinking the cup," in addition to the symbolic meaning it has for Mark, is here presented as a decision to obey Jesus and share in his life and saving mission.

Any coldness that might be perceived in the call to obedience is removed by the warmth of the Emmanuel theme: Jesus is the incarnate proof of God's desire to live among his

---

[13]Senior, *The Passion of Jesus*, 67.

people, and he will remain with the Church until the end of history. He is present now in a special way in the Eucharist, which is a foreshadowing of the eternal banquet to come. Drink the cup with me now, Jesus says, and I will drink it with you from now on in my Father's kingdom.

8

The Eucharist of Luke

Luke is the third Synoptic evangelist, but his Gospel presents a situation different from that of Mark and Matthew for two reasons. In the narration of the Last Supper Luke is closer to Paul than to Mark/ Matthew; he is not, like Matthew, simply adjusting Mark's narrative to his own traditions. We recognize Luke's dependence on Mark, but also his use of a narrative tradition which Paul also used and of other independent material. Besides, in the Acts of the Apostles Luke has written a sequel to his Gospel; in his story of the birth and early development of the Church we can expect some light on the post-Easter Eucharist.

Several unique stresses in the Lucan writings must be addressed in any examination of the Lucan theology of the Eucharist. The feeding of the five thousand is recorded in Luke (9:12-17), but not the feeding of the four thousand. However, Luke tells of several meals of Jesus both before and after the Last Supper which seem to have eucharistic overtones. Meals and food are more of a pervasive theme than in Mark and Matthew. Luke records the words of institution, including the cup and its interpretation (in fact, there are two cups in Luke), and he has Jesus' prayer in the Garden that the cup might pass, but he omits the story of James and John and does not develop the theme of the cup. The doctrine of expiatory suffering and death is practically omitted except for the traditional references in the Supper account.

In our examination of Luke's eucharistic themes, we will first look at his use of food and eating, then proceed to particular meals, leading up to an investigation of Luke's presentation of the Last Supper.

Food

Robert Karris has catalogued references to the food theme in Luke's Gospel, finding at least one instance in every chapter.[1] This theme follows through in the Acts of the Apostles, where the resolution of the debate about baptism of non-Jews is set in motion by the question of food (Acts 10:10-16). Karris notes two overarching food themes in the Gospel, Jesus as the one in whom God feeds his hungry creation, and Jesus as God's messenger of justice who is put to death because of his openness in sharing food with everyone without exception.

The theme of God's lavish feeding of the needy is established in Mary's canticle early in the Gospel: "He has filled the hungry with good things, and the rich he has sent empty away"(1:53). The Hebrew Bible had spoken of the eschatological kingdom in terms of plenty of food and drink for the needy poor:

> Ho, everyone who thirsts, come to the waters;
> and he who has no money, buy and eat!
> Come, buy wine and milk without money and without price
> (Is 55:1; see Ps 22:26).

Lazarus, in Jesus' story of the rich man and the beggar, gives concrete expression to this theme. He was excluded from the rich man's table here on earth, but is pictured as sitting with Abraham at the heavenly table (16:23; see 13:28-29).

Eschatological preparedness is described in the image of the return of the master from a wedding (12:35-40). The key sentence here, unique to Luke's account, is "he will gird himself and have them sit at table, and he will come and serve them"(v 37). This master makes an extraordinary impression by his

---

[1] *Luke: Artist and Theologian*, pp. 49-51.

humility and service.[2] In John's instruction to the crowd who ask "What then shall we do?," a sign of repentance will be the sharing of food with those in need (3:11). Conversion will bring the disciple to imitate Jesus who imitates the Father in his generosity to the poor and outcast. The various incidents in which Jesus reveals the openhandedness of his Father climax in the eucharistic institution with its eschatological promise, which is expanded in Luke's version (22:16-18).

Jesus expressed the willingness of the Father to save his people, all who would accept salvation, by his willingness to share food with everyone and by his own open hospitality. The importance of sharing a meal together is lost on most of us in our modern fast-food society, but in Jesus' world table fellowship set up an intimate relationship. It was not to be taken lightly. There were religious rules to protect the integrity of the fellowship of the faithful Jewish community.

By eating with those who were considered sinners, Jesus deeply offended the sensibilities of the religious leaders. This practice was interpreted as an act of apostasy. For eating with outcasts, Jesus was criticized as "a glutton and a drunkard" (7:34; see Dt 21:20). Luke makes this a major theme, portraying Jesus as the prophet whose pattern of eating and drinking with sinners is an acted parable proclaiming God's offer of life to all. "The table becomes a place where human need meets divine grace."[3] Jesus arouses astonishment by eating with the tax collectors Levi and Zacchaeus (6:29-30; 19:5-7) and with the sinful woman in Simon's house (7:36-39). But Luke makes it clear also that Jesus was not doctrinaire in his concern for the outcast. He ate with the rich and powerful, too (14:1). The Last Supper is the final meal in a series during Jesus' ministry. There he teaches his disciples how they are to act after he is gone by his interpretation of the bread and wine, by his last instructions, and by sharing table fellowship with his betrayer.

[2]P.E. Deterding points out that the table service of the master is a foreshadowing of the Last Supper (see especially 22:27): "Eschatological and Eucharistic Motifs in Luke 12:35-40," *Concordia Journal* 5 (1979) 85-94.

[3]Paul S. Minear, "Some Glimpses of Luke's Sacramental Theology," *Worship* 44 (1970) 322–331, 325.

The incident about the dispute over fasting from Mark fits very well with Luke's presentation of the banqueting Jesus (5:33-39; Mk 2:18-22). Jesus is questioned about the fact that he has not required of his disciples the fasting that John expected of his disciples. Jesus couches his answer in the imagery of the wedding banquet. He is not hostile to the idea of fasting but he is teaching the conviviality of the kingdom. "The day will come when the bridegroom is taken away from them, and then they will fast in those days (v 35)." Fasting can be a very wholesome practice but it may serve pride and provoke judgment and separation from others (Lk 18:9-14). Jesus is more concerned to accentuate the positive in establishing an open fellowship of love through his meals with the outcasts.[4]

Meals

The food theme is expressed in different ways in Luke's writing, but we perceive the evangelist's perspective on the Eucharist especially in a series of meals. The first of these is taken over from Mark, the meal with the tax collector Levi (5:27-32). The story is in a section dealing with calls to discipleship. Luke stresses the radical nature of this following of Jesus, as he does elsewhere (5:11; 14:33), adding to the Marcan text, "He left everything" (v 28). Heinz Schürmann has noted that the direction of the question about eating with sinners toward the disciples rather than to Jesus (v 30; Mk 2:16) is meant to apply the scene to the post-Easter Eucharist.[5] The message seems to be that Jesus will be present as a guest where his disciples share the Eucharist, and as converted sinners they must remain open to fellowship with other sinners who also need the physician.[6] Jesus' fellowship with sinners is a

---

[4]Joseph F. Wimmer, *Fasting in the New Testament: A Study in Bibilical Theology* (Theological Inquiries; New York: Paulist, 1982) 112.

[5]*Das Lukasevangelium*, I (HTKNT 3/1; Freiburg: Herder, 1969) 290.

[6]Joachim Wanke interprets this scene as meaning that only *converted* sinners are worthy to sit at table with Jesus. Of all the evangelists this seems least true for Luke, who makes it a point to note the presence of the betrayer (who could be any of the participants) right after the words of institution at the Last Supper (22:21):

call to repentance, a point that Luke makes specific (v 32; see Mk 2:17).

In another meal story (7:36-50), the host is not a tax collector (=sinner), but a Pharisee (=righteous person). But the focus of the table talk is the same: How can Jesus associate with sinners? Simon, blind to his own debt, cannot see the woman as she really is. But Jesus can see by the love she expresses that she has already been forgiven (v 47). This point is obscured in the RSV but brought out in the Jerusalem Bible: "I tell you that her sins, her many sins, must have been forgiven her, or she would not have shown such great love." Jesus sees her repentance and confirms her forgiveness. The new question raises the level of the discussion: "Who is this who even forgives sins?" (v 49). Jesus is willing to eat with sinners, whether they acknowledge their sin or not, in hopes of bringing them to forgiveness.

The story of the feeding of the five thousand (Lk 9:11-17) is very little changed from Mark. The eucharistic overtone is present as in the other Gospels, and may be heightened by the use of the title "the Twelve" (v 12), which is the term associated with table serving in Acts (6:2). But the principal change is in the context. In Luke, this passage leads up to the question about Jesus' identity and Peter's declaration that he is "the Christ of God" (v 20). Jesus' hospitality (he "welcomed them": v 11), his preaching and healing, and his feeding of the people are signs by which Peter recognizes the Master's true identity.

The parable of the Great Banquet from Q (Lk 14:15-24; Mt 22:1-14) is situated in Luke within a meal setting unique to the Third Evangelist. The meal in this Pharisee's house recalls themes presented in other table scenes: the leaders' imposing of impossible burdens on the people and their love of places of honor (11:37-52), and the welcoming of guests who cannot repay the gesture (15:20-24). Jesus overturns usual human expectation in his words and actions at table: take the lowest seat; invite the poor, the weak, the handicapped. Besides reflecting the Lucan emphasis on openness to the poor, this incident shows Jesus removing barriers between high and low,

Beobachtungen zum Eucharistieverständnis des Lukas (Erfurter Theologische Schriften 8; Leipzig: St. Benno, 1973) 57.

rich and poor, powerful and weak. Later in Acts, the axiom that "God shows no partiality" (10:34) will help to launch the universal mission of the Church.

A remark of one of the table guests turns the conversation to the theme of the heavenly banquet and serves as an introduction to the parable Luke has in common with Matthew:[7] "Blessed is he who shall eat bread in the kingdom of God!" (14:15). Jesus takes this as the cue to puncture the complacency he detects in this pious proverb. The Pharisee and his guests feel themselves protected by their observance of religious rules and have already been taken aback by Jesus' freedom to break the rituals for the sake of a higher good (vv 1-6).

Jesus tells a story which contains a warning for those who might not hear the call to the great supper because of a casual, self-protective attitude. "None of those men who were invited will taste my banquet" (v 24). By the time this parable was incorporated into Luke's Gospel, sharing table fellowship with Jesus in the Eucharist was a regular feature of Christian worship. Complacency was still a possibility, and in a new way: we share the eucharistic table with the risen Lord; surely he will not reject us. But just a few paragraphs earlier Jesus had warned in another parable: "You will begin to say, 'We ate and drank in your presence, and you taught in our streets.' But we will say, 'I tell you, I do not know where you come from'" (13:26-37). Immediately after the parable of the great banquet, Jesus describes the cost of discipleship in stark terms (14:25-33). Those who share the eucharistic table must decide whether they are willing to make the commitment their fellowship with the Lord implies.

The meal scenes continue after the death and resurrection of Jesus. In Luke's Gospel and Acts it is very natural to read about fellowship meals among Jesus' disciples after the events of Holy Week and to learn of his presence with them at table. Table fellowship was a regular occurrence before the resurrec-

---

[7]The parable of the Great Banquet is narrated with significant differences by the two evangelists. A third form of the parable appears in the non-canonical Gospel of Thomas and seems to come from a more primitive stage of transmission. See Joseph A. Fitzmyer, *The Gospel According to Luke X-XXIV* (AB 28A; Garden City: Doubleday, 1985), 105-54.

tion, and it continues afterward, but in a new way. One of the most memorable Easter stories is that of the appearance of the two dejected disciples on their way to Emmaus (24:13-35). Jesus explains how the Scriptures have been fulfilled in his ministry and his death. The two invite him to stay with them for the evening meal. Assuming the role of the host, Jesus "took the bread and blessed, and broke it, and gave it to them" (v 30). Their eyes were opened and they recognized him in "the breaking of the bread" (v 35). Joachim Wanke has found the prevailing theological theme of the post-Easter Eucharist in Luke to be the presence of the risen Lord among his followers.[8] The sequel to this story, with its stress on the reality of Jesus' body, is designed to show that the risen Christ is none other than the Jesus of Nazareth they have known (vv 38-43). At Emmaus, Jesus performs the ritual that is recognized as his signature and then, when he is recognized, disappears. From now on, the Lord will be present with his disciples in the breaking of the bread, but he will no longer be visible.

In three places the Acts of the Apostles uses eucharistic language to describe meals (2:42-47; 20:7-11; 27:33-36). There is doubt among some scholars that these meals are meant as eucharistic, but the references to the "breaking of the bread" in the summary description of Jerusalem community life (Acts 2:42, 46) and in the Troas narrative (20:7) are too pointed for a careful writer like Luke. The repetition of the familiar "took . . . gave thanks . . . broke . . ." in the ship off Malta (27:35) is a reminder of the example of Jesus at the multiplication of loaves and at the Last Supper, though the meal is probably not a Eucharist.[9]

It has been proposed that the "breaking of the bread" in Acts 2:42, 46 means either an ordinary meal or a Christian love-feast (*agapē*: see Jude 12). But the term never refers to a whole meal in Jewish usage, and the circumstances of Emmaus

[8] *Beobachtungen*, 67. See also his study, *Die Emmäuserzählung: Eine redaktions-geschichtliche Untersuchung zu Lk 24, 13-35* (Erfurter Theologische Studien 31; Leipzig: St. Benno, 1973).

[9] R.D. Richardson argues that it is a liturgical rite in "The Place of Luke in the Eucharistic Tradition," *Studia Evangelica*, TU 73 (Berlin: Akadamie-Verlag, 1959) 663-75, 671-72.

militate against its being only an *agapē*. Joachim Jeremias has suggested that the word *koinōnia* (fellowship) in 2:42 might be better translated as "table-fellowship"; and that this refers to the love-feast that preceded the Eucharist.[10] Therefore this summary verse would be describing a primitive order of celebration. P.H. Menoud finds the distinction between Eucharist and *agapē* in the "breaking of bread" and the partaking of food "with glad and generous hearts" in verse 46, but in a different order.[11]

Other clues to early practice may be discerned in verse 46. Is it possible that already in these earliest times there was a daily ("day by day") Eucharist? The reference is too scant to interpret with certainty. It does, however, challenge the position that the early Christians celebrated the Eucharist only once a year at the Passover. Luke is at pains to record the uninterrupted temple observance of the faithful Jews who made up the Christian community (see also 3:1; 21:20-25). Perhaps this Jewish observance had a role in changing the principal day of worship from Saturday to Sunday. The Jewish converts were able to offer Eucharist only after the Sabbath was over (sundown Saturday). Then began the "first day of the week," the day of the resurrection (Acts 20:7; see Mk 16:1-2).

The report of the all-night gathering at Troas in Acts 20:7-12 is our first clear witness to the celebration of the Eucharist on Sunday. Other New Testament references to the "first day of the week" (1 Cor 16:2) or the "Lord's day" (Rev 1:10) are not specific. Paul's lengthy sermon takes its toll on the young man Eutychus, who falls asleep and topples from the third story to his death. Paul calmly brings the youth back to life, breaks bread, and continues preaching. Wanke sees in this episode another example of Luke's emphasis on the saving presence of the risen Lord in the Eucharist. He points out that Jesus as savior is a major theme of Acts (4:12; 5:31; 13:23), and that the meal with eucharistic overtones on the ship is a harbinger of

---

[10]Such an order has been suggested for 1 Cor 11:18-34 and Didache IX-X. See the discussion in Jeremias, *Eucharistic Words*, 118-22.

[11]"The Acts of the Apostles and the Eucharist,'" *Jesus Christ and the Faith* (Pittsburgh: Pickwick, 1978), 88.

rescue from disaster (27:33-36). Though Jesus is not mentioned specifically, the healing and saving aura of these two meals may be assumed as a precision for the Eucharist of the theme of Jesus' saving presence in Paul's ministry and throughout the life of the Church. In connection with this, both passages also show Paul allaying the fear of the participants.[12]

To summarize important elements in the pre- and post-Easter meals which throw light on Luke's theology of the Eucharist:

1)Jesus is present, taking an active role whether as guest or host. He is concerned about those at table with him and serves them, responding to their need for food, healing, teaching, or correction.

2) He welcomes all, sinner or righteous, poor or rich. He does not fear being compromised by the company he keeps; and he overturns human expectations by expressing his own unique values.

3) His meals are harbingers of the banquet to be shared in the kingdom of God. Those who share God's gifts now and hope in his promises must not let complacency rob them of the fulfillment.

4)The light of Easter helps the Christian community understand Scripture's witness to Jesus; the disciples recognize the risen Lord in the breaking of the bread.

Last Supper (22:14-38)

In Luke's Gospel the Last Supper is the final installment in a series of meals which reveal Jesus' identity and purpose during his ministry. This is the only occasion, aside from the feeding of the five thousand in the wilderness, when Jesus is the host. Prepared by the importance of the table talk at other meals, we are not surprised to find that the dialogue is expanded in Luke's version of the Supper. This makes his meal narration about twice as long as that in Mark and Matthew.[13] Luke has

[12]See Wanke, *Beobachtungen*, 22-24.

[13]Richardson sees this expansion as representing a stage of development towards the lengthy farewell discourse of John's Gospel: "The Place of Luke," 669.

cast his narrative into the form of the farewell speech, a convention well established in biblical literature, from Jacob (Gen 47-50) to Paul (Acts 20:17-35). The departing leader gathers his primary community for the last time, predicts what will happen after he is gone, and exhorts his followers about their behavior after his departure.[14]

In the preparation for the Supper (22:7-14), Luke follows Mark with only minor alterations. The two disciples in Mk 14:13 are named here as Peter and John, the two who will emerge as leading figures in the Acts of the Apostles (3:1-11; 8:14). But after this, there are two significant structural changes in the Lucan Supper. The mention of the betrayer is transferred after the sharing of the bread and wine. The eschatological saying comes before the words of institution rather than afterward as in Mark. Though all the accounts reflect the life of the community in which they were passed down, Luke is in a more conscious way addressing the situation of the Church between resurrection and parousia. Dennis Sweetland has summarized this thrust of the Lucan narrative:

> In the absence of Jesus (vv 15-18) the community, united through the Lord's Supper to the Risen One who gives himself as Servant (19-20), is a fellowship which cannot abide a betrayer (21-23) and has a legacy of service (24-27). Though ordered to the heavenly banquet (28-30) it must undergo strife (35-38). However, it has the assurance of the support of the Risen One who strengthens Peter, and through the faithful disciples, supports the community (31-32).[15]

The Supper begins with an expression of Jesus' deep feeling about sharing this last meal with his closest disciples: "I have

---

[14]See the chapter, "Jesus' Farewell Speech (Lk 22:14-38)," in Jerome Neyrey, *The Passion According to Luke: A Redaction Study of Luke's Soteriology* (Theological Inquiries; New York: Paulist, 1985) 5-48; and Charles H. Talbert, *Reading Luke: A Literary and Theological Commentary on the Third Gospel* (New York: Crossroad, 1982), 207-08.

[15]"The Lord's Supper," 23.

earnestly desired to eat this passover with you before I suffer" (v 15). The meal is immediately couched in an expectation of Jesus' death. This is expressed again in verses 16-18 where Jesus speaks of not eating or drinking "until the kingdom of God comes." Placing the eschatological promise before the sharing of the bread and wine instead of afterward (Mk 14:25) has been interpreted as implying that the Last Supper is already a meal for the realized kingdom.[16] But the easiest meaning is, as in the other Synoptics, that Jesus is sharing this intimate kind of meal with the disciples for the last time before his death.[17] He will share with them again when the kingdom is realized in his resurrection. For Luke, this means both in the life of the Church (7:28) and in the heavenly banquet (13:28-29). The Lucan emphasis here is on the Eucharist of the Church which Jesus will soon share with his Christian disciples: at Emmaus, in Jerusalem, and elsewhere.

The context of the institution narrative is altered in Luke by the omission of the Marcan cup-theme and the ransom saying earlier in the Gospel. The doctrine of the atoning death is still present in the traditional words "given for you" and "poured out for you" (vv 19-20), but the themes of fellowship and service color Luke's presentation of the doctrine. "Go and prepare the passover *for us*, that *we* may eat it"(v 8; contrast Mk 14:12). "I have earnestly desired to eat this passover *with you*"(v 15). "I am among you as one who serves"(v 27). In Luke's theology, Jesus' death is the acceptance of obedient humiliation by God's Servant (*pais*: Acts 2:13, 26), an act which breaks the hold of sin and death (Acts 2:24). His death is the ultimate act of service.[18] He gives this gift to his disciples proleptically by sharing with them the bread and wine, his body and blood. "Do this in remembrance of me"(v 19) means as it does for Paul, not only performing the ritual or recalling a

[16]*Ibid.*

[17]See Fitzmyer, *Luke X-XXIV*, 1396. The placing of the first cup and the words accompanying it is probably not a Lucan decision but simply the order in the independent tradition he had received (more primitive than Mark's at this point), reflecting the structure of the Jewish meal.

[18]See Richard Glöckner, *Die Verkündigung des Heils beim Evangelisten Lukas* (Walberberger Studien 9; Mainz: Matthias Grünewald, 1976), 177-80.

historical memory but making the same self-gift that Jesus made. But the particular context of fellowship and service gives the words "new covenant in my blood" an added nuance not found in First Corinthians.

The warning about the betrayer, moved after the words of institution, and the wrangling among the disciples over their greatness are particularly chilling as immediate sequels to the cup-word. Luke does not name the betrayer (vv 21-23). None of the participants (at the Last Supper or in the later Eucharist) knows who the betrayer might be. It might be any of them (or us). This can be understood as a warning for the Lucan community about complacency; but it also bears witness to Jesus' continuing openness and hospitality despite the betrayal of a table companion. By offering himself for all without self-concern Jesus reveals what it means to act as a servant.

Luke has transferred the dispute over greatness (vv 24-30) from its place in the journey to Jerusalem in Mark's Gospel (10:35-45) and also expanded the involvement from James and John to all the apostles. At this point the apostles are not asking for a place at his right and left hand. They do not have to. Jesus is promising them a place on twelve thrones, judging the twelve tribes of Israel (v 30). The instruction is addressed to those who have in fact become the leaders of the Christian community and to their successors. Instead of Mark's "Whoever would be first among you must be slave of all" (Mk 10:44), Luke has "Let the *leader (hēgoumenos)* be as one who serves" (v 26). Jesus' companions at table cannot have been too upset by the thought of the betrayal in their midst, because immediately they fell into bickering over their own importance and what they would derive from their nearness to Jesus.

The final two pericopes of the Last Supper narrative are meant to give confidence (though not over-confidence) for Christian leaders during the time of persecution to come. Satan has "demanded to have *you* (plural: v 31)," but Jesus' prayer will support Simon Peter ("you" singular: v 32) so that he may strengthen the others. This role of Peter is portrayed in Peter's witness and missionary preaching in the first chapters of Acts. Jesus warns his followers that hard times are coming, of which his death will be the first installment (vv 35-38). They must be prepared. They misunderstand now (v 38) but will later comprehend that their strength and protection comes from Jesus, who will renew his covenant with them in the post-Easter Eucharist. Jesus will not distance himself from them because they fail him. The keynote of his ministry, and especially his table fellowship, has been "He was reckoned with transgressors" (Is 53:12; Lk 22:37), both by his own desire and the will of his persecutors (see 23: 32). And he will continue to share his life with sinners in the kingdom meals of the time of the Church.

Summary

Luke's food and meals motif provides a broader canvas for his eucharistic teaching than is found in the other Gospels. The meals during the ministry look forward to the Last Supper and the post-Easter meals, and all of them have implications for the Eucharist of the Church. The open table fellowship of Jesus is a parable of God's offer of life and salvation to all. Jesus does not turn away from the outcast, the sinner, the betrayer; nor is he less open to the (self-) righteous because of his concern for the weak. His presence at table creates a bond which will become a new covenant bond at the Last Supper. The meals portray Jesus as teacher and healer, the one who is willing to forgive and reconcile. He offers hope to the humble and overturns the complacency of the proud.

In Luke's Eucharist the cup does not have the symbolic weight it carries for Mark. The body "given for you" and the blood "poured out for you" represent Jesus' ultimate act of service, accepting humiliation to the death in an obedient submission which breaks the bonds of sin. This is the basis of a new covenant relationship which relies on his presence and support and calls for imitation. The Eucharist looks backward in remembrance and forward in expectation to the banquet of the fulfilled kingdom.

9

The Eucharist of John

The latest of the writings considered in this study, and the last to be reviewed, differs considerably from the others in its presentation of the place of the Eucharist in the Christian life. The Gospel of John has no institution narrative at the Last Supper, nor does it use titles like "Lord's Supper" or "Breaking of the Bread." John does, however, communicate eucharistic teaching which has been very influential in Christian tradition. Similarly, though John presents no command of Jesus to baptize and no baptism ritual, his Gospel is rich in baptismal teaching. In fact, John is generally seen today as the most "sacramental" of all the Gospels.[1] Visible events and material things become signs of divine realities. The handful of miracles John records are not *dynameis* (works of power) as in the Synoptics but *sēmeia* (signs). Water becomes "living water" (Jn 4:10), sight means faith (9:36-37), bread points to "the bread of life" (6:34-35).

One of the few episodes of Jesus' public life that John has preserved along with the Synoptics is that of the multiplication of the loaves. John recognized the eucharistic theme in this account, but instead of using it as a foreshadowing of the institution later in the Gospel, he lets it serve as the keynote to a chapter with a long discourse by Jesus on the bread of life (6:1-15; 25-59). Later, the image of the vine will be another

[1]See the section on "Sacraments" in the commentary by C. K. Barrett, *The Gospel According to St. John: An Introduction with Commentary and Notes on the Greek Text* (London: SPCK, 1962), 69-71.

vehicle for eucharistic teaching (15:1-8). Why is John's approach to this central reality so different from that of the other writers? There is no doubt that by this time the Eucharist was a regular and vital part of the faith life of his community as of the other Christian communities. The institution account was not omitted because it was not known. What was John trying to communicate about the Eucharist that led him to avoid its mention in the account of the Last Supper?

John's treatment of the Eucharist, as of everything else, flows from his doctrine of the Incarnation. At the beginning of the Fourth Gospel, Jesus is introduced to the reader not as a baby born in Bethlehem (which is also an incarnational approach) but as the eternal word of the Father made flesh (1:14). Jesus is the word of God who has come down from heaven (3:13) and who through his life, death and resurrection draws all humanity to himself (12:32), thereby opening the way to eternal life. Through the symbols of light, water, bread, the vine, John shows Jesus as the response to the deepest aspirations of humanity.[2] John uses the word *sarx* (flesh) instead of *sōma* (body) when speaking of the word's becoming human and when speaking of the eucharistic bread of life (6:51). *Sōma* means a body tangible to sense, while *sarx* implies human nature in its completeness.[3]

The saving death of Jesus is crucial to the work of atonement in John as well as in Paul. It is the "hour" for which Jesus was always preparing (2:4; 12:27). At Jesus' death, blood and water flowed from his side, symbolic of baptism and Eucharist, now the channels of salvation and life in the Church. But the Eucharist is not understood as a rite focusing on the commemoration of the death of Jesus as in Paul. It is rather interpreted in terms of food and drink for eternal life.[4] The Eucharist is a continuation in our time of the power Jesus

---

[2] André Feuillet, *Johannine Studies* (Staten Island: Alba House, 1965), 125.

[3] G. H. C. MacGregor, "The Eucharist in the Fourth Gospel," *NTS* 9 (1962-63) 111-19, 116-17. See also Johannes Betz, *Eucharistie In der Schrift und Patristik* (Handbuch der Dogmengeschichte IV; Freiburg: Herder, 1979) 22-24.

[4] Raymond E. Brown, *The Community of the Beloved Disciple: The Life, Loves, and Hates of an Individual Church in New Testament Times* (New York: Paulist, 1979), 79, n. 145.

exhibited during his earthly ministry when he fed and healed the people. Thus, rather than connecting the Eucharist to the Last Supper, John has references to it throughout the story of Jesus' life: the wine at Cana (2:1-12; possibly), the loaves of multiplication (6:1-13), the vine and the branches (15:1-8). John did not want to isolate the institution of the Eucharist as a final mandate from the Lord, but to show it as flowing from everything he said and did as the word become flesh so that we might have eternal life. He also was wary of making the Eucharist seem only like a Church action mandated by Christ; Jesus himself is at the heart of it as the source of God's life. Union with Jesus, not only with the Church, is fundamental.[5]

On another level, the Eucharist is a radical call to faith. The Incarnation is a great offense to "enlightened" sensibilities; surely God could not and would not stoop that low. This is the objection of Docetists from John's time to our own. The requirement to "eat the flesh" of the Son of man continues the offense of the Incarnation, sacramentalizing it in a ritual act.

The Johannine perspective is clarified further by contrasting it with Paul's eucharistic teaching in First Corinthians 11, where the Lord's Supper is performed as a proclamation of the death of Jesus and in obedience to the command, "Do this in remembrance of me."[6] The emphasis of Paul is on an action performed by the community, the essential community act which brings the saving event of Christ's death into the midst of the assembled faithful. This act is consummated in the eating and drinking of the body and blood of the Lord; the emphasis is on the action and its community effect, not on the benefit of the divine food for the individual participant. This benefit is not denied, but is not stated. The one loaf and the one cup express and strengthen the unity of the body of Christ (1 Cor 10:17).

A major theme of First Corinthians, as already noted, is Paul's insistence that members of the community learn how to subordinate their personal interests to the good of the group.

---

[5] *Ibid.*, 86.

[6] In what follows I am indebted to the insights of Thomas Worden, "The Holy Eucharist in St. John," *Scripture* 15 (1963), 97-99.

In terms of the Eucharist this means that they must be aware of the meaning of their participation in the community action of the Eucharist: when they partake of the bread and wine it must be more than a convivial activity: not just any meal, but the Lord's Supper. They are sharing in the body and blood of Christ and if they do so carelessly will be guilty of profaning the body and blood of the Lord (11:27)

John is writing almost forty years later than Paul. He is not so concerned about the meaning of the eucharistic action, which by this time is standard knowledge in the Christian communities. John concentrates his attention on the meaning and consequences of the Eucharist for the individual participant. This development was in part a response to the delay of the parousia. When Paul wrote to the Corinthians, expectation of the early return of the Lord was very much alive (see I Cor 15:51-52). The eschatological thrust of the Eucharist was dominant as Christians shared the Lord's Supper in anticipation of his return (11:26). The fact that some members of the community had already died before the parousia was a problem for Paul, and he seems to interpret their death as a judgment on selfishness in the celebration of the Eucharist (11:29-30).

The Corinthians might have argued another way. If our brothers and sisters are becoming sick and dying before the Lord's coming, what good is the Eucharist doing them? Why not gain what we can personally while we are still here: a good meal, prestige, the support of a small, like-minded group? By John's time many more had died, including the leaders and many other recognized saints. How had the Eucharist benefitted them? John develops precisely the point of the present and future benefit of sharing at the Lord's table: "He who eats my flesh and drinks my blood has eternal life, and I will raise him up at the last day" (Jn 6:54).

The Bread of Life (6:1-71)

The Eucharistic teaching of John is found principally in Chapter Six, where the evangelist records the episode of the multiplication of the loaves and follows with the long discourse of Jesus on the bread of life. The chapter begins with crowds swarming around Jesus because of the healings he has performed. They are eager and urgent, hoping that Jesus will be a savior for them, perhaps even the Messiah. John uses this context to show who Jesus is, and to reveal that the reason he has come into the world may be summed up in his offer of himself to the people: he has come to be the bread of life. As such, he will respond to all their real needs in the ultimately satisfying way. The bread of life theme is larger than the Eucharist, but the Eucharist is a key aspect, the sacramental climax of the mission of the word of God to the world.

As so often in John, there are misunderstandings and different levels of meaning at work. The people follow Jesus because of the signs he is working (v 2), but their interest is all on the material level. They have no true insight into the signs. The words of Jesus bring out this misunderstanding: "You seek me, not because you saw signs, but because you ate your fill of the loaves" (v 26). In their misguided zeal, the people respond to the feeding by trying to make Jesus king. They hope that he will be a Davidic leader who will fulfill their material needs and respond to their political aspirations. But Jesus urges them to the deeper level of spiritual food and eternal life.[7]

John tells us that it is near the feast of Passover. This detail is lacking in the Synoptics, though Mark mentions that there is "green grass," a sign of springtime (Mk 6:39). Whether or not this is a historical remembrance, the mention of Passover illuminates John's theme here.[8] The Passover liturgy of the Jews mentioned both the giving of manna through Moses and the crossing of the Red Sea, two historical precedents which provide a salvation history context for the feeding story and the bread of life discourse, and for the story of the walking on the water. The Passover is also the context for the Last Supper and for the death of Jesus (13:1; 19:14).

Like the Synoptic accounts, John's narrative of the multi-plication of the loaves shows signs of adaptation to the

[7]Jean Giblet, "The Eucharist in St. John's Gospel: John 6," *Concilium* 10 (Dec., 1968), 33-35.

[8]Contrast John's attention to this detail with the vague setting of the healing at the Sheep gate: "a feast of the Jews" (5:1).

Eucharistic theme. John has many similarities to the other accounts, but also some differences. He uses the evocative words *eucharistēsas* (having given thanks) and *klasmatōn* (fragments), but omits the glance toward heaven and the breaking of the bread. A special feature is the distribution of the loaves by Jesus himself (v 11), as in the Synoptic account of the Last Supper.[9] The Johannine account also shows Jesus instructing the disciples to gather the fragments, a eucharistic theme current at the time, as is witnessed by the prayer of the Didache, "As this broken bread (*to klasma*) was scattered upon the mountains, but was brought together and became one, so let your Church be gathered from the ends of the earth into your kingdom" (IX, 4).[10]

The incident of the loaves is a sign of the deeper and richer kind of feeding Jesus will reveal in the bread of life discourse (vv 35-58). Instead of turning to this discourse immediately, John recounts the story of the walking on the water. This story was already in the tradition at this point (see Mk 6:32-52), but in John's presentation, the walking on the water finds its focus in Jesus' declaration, "I am he (*egō eimi*); do not be afraid" (v 20). In four places, the Johannine Jesus makes *egō eimi* statements in an absolute sense: e.g., "Before Abraham was, I am" (8:58; see 8:24, 28; 13:19). This reflects the Old Testament and rabbinic usage for the divine name; these words on the lips of Jesus imply his divinity.[11] The implication of divinity may be muted in verse 20, but the overtone is there. This provides a backdrop for Jesus' claim that he is the bread of life.

The unity of John 6 has been a matter of considerable discussion. It is typical to see a sapiential theme of Jesus the bread of life in verse 35-50, and either the heightening of this theme or the change to a specifically eucharistic theme in verses 51-58. There is the further problem of the relationship of verses 60-71 to the rest of the chapter. After insisting on the

[9]See the chart comparing the four accounts in Brown, *The Gospel According to John I-XII*, 240-43. A convincing argument for the independence of John's account is presented by Edwin D. Johnston, "The Johannine Version of the Feeding of the Five Thousand—An Independent Tradition?," *NTS* 8 (1961-62), 151-54.

[10]C.F.D. Moule, "A Note on Didache IX 4," *JTS* 6 (1955) 240-43.

[11]Brown, *The Gospel According to John I-XII*, Appendix IV, 533-538.

necessity of "eating the flesh of the son of man" (v 53), Jesus in verse 63 says: "It is the spirit that gives life, the flesh is of no avail." These last verses jar with those immediately preceding and are best understood as a continuation of the dialogue in verses 35-50. Verses 51-58 are an insertion by the author or the Johannine school meant to carry the point about the bread of life through to its eucharistic conclusion.[12]

Though the feeding miracle introduced the theme of the chapter, that incident is not mentioned again after verse 26. The loaves give way to the theme of manna in the desert. The Jews quote the statement, "He gave them bread from heaven to eat," a composite of various Old Testament passages (e.g. Ex 16:15; Ps 78:24). Jesus takes up this text (v 32) and makes it the focus of the whole discourse.

When Jesus calls himself the "bread of life" (v 35), he is designating himself as the wisdom of God come to earth. More is meant here than that Jesus' brings the true teaching from God. In saying "He who comes to me shall not hunger, and he who believes in me shall never thirst," Jesus echoes the words of divine wisdom in Sirach, "Those who eat me will hunger for more, and those who drink me will thirst for more" (24:21). A taste of God's wisdom creates more and more of a hunger, but in Jesus the hunger can be satisfied. John's Incarnation theme is to the fore here: Jesus has come to the world to give true life, eternal life, to God's children. The manna could not satisfy this need: "Your fathers ate the manna in the wilderness, and they died. This is the bread which comes down from heaven, that a man may eat of it and not die" (vv 49-50).

Whatever one's theory of editing, Chapter 6 as we have it is united around the theme of the bread of life; even the verses which are primarily sapiential have an underlying current of eucharistic meaning. But the Eucharist theme emerges clearly in verse 51, where Jesus describes himself as the *living* bread

---

[12]Brown, *ibid.,* 287, proposes that this material was transferred here from the Johannine account of the institution at the Last Supper. Others argue that vv 51-58 were added by a redactor: e. g., Urban C. von Wahlde, *"Wiederaufnahme* as a Mark of Redaction in Jn 6:51-58," *Bib* 64 (1983) 542-49. But the original unity of the discourse is still defended, most recently for example by Joseph A. Grassi, "Eating Jesus' Flesh and Drinking his Blood: The Centrality and Meaning of John 6:51-58," *BTB* 17 (1987) 24-30.

which gives eternal life. Many commentators have glimpsed an institution text here, noting that "The bread which I shall give for the life of the world is my flesh" is close to the Lucan formula "This is my body which is given for you" (Lk 22:19). John has adapted the theme to his own purposes by the use of *sarx* (flesh) in place of the Synoptic and Pauline *sōma* (body). Up till now, the word *sarx* has appeared only once in the Fourth Gospel (3:6) since the programmatic statement: "The word became flesh" (1:14). Now, in a few sentences, *sarx* appears six times, half the total uses in the Gospel. The purpose of Jesus' coming to the world is climaxed in a crucial way in "eating his flesh." The image is harsh, but even harsher for the Hebrew mind would be the command to drink blood (vv 53-56), something that was forbidden by God (Gen 9:4). The word used for "eat" in verses 56-57 (*trōgein*) has the vulgar connotation of "gnaw." Perhaps this severe imagery was a direct challenge to the Docetists who denied the humanity of Jesus and therefore gave a metaphorical interpretation of the eucharistic elements. But mainly it is John's way of saying that the Eucharist makes available to the individual believer personal union with Jesus in his divine mission of salvation. It is an action of the community, but it is at the same time the means by which each believer ratifies and renews the personal union of faith with Christ, by sacramentally eating the flesh of the Son of man and drinking his blood.

The word "faith" alerts us to an essential dimension of this chapter, as of John's entire Gospel.[13] Faith is the primary factor in discipleship (3:16), and it is also the fundamental attitude for openness to Jesus as the bread of life. The dialogue with the Jews revolves around the question of faith (6:29-30, 36). Jesus will be the bread of life whether in the sapiential sense or in the eucharistic sense only for those who accept the invitation of the Father (v 44) and respond in faith. Otherwise the bread and wine will be signs only on a superficial level. "This is the will of my Father, that *every one who sees the Son and believes in him* should have eternal life; and I will raise him up at the last day" (v 40). The italicized words are replaced in

---

[13]The verb *pisteuein* (to believe) appears 98 times in the Gospel of John.

verse 54 by "he who eats my flesh and drinks my blood," implying that the act of faith is expressed in the "sign" language of the eucharistic meal. The bread of life is the source of eternal life now and carries the promise of resurrection at the parousia.

Jesus goes on to say that the believer who eats his flesh and drinks his blood "abides in me, and I in him" (v 56). The word *menein* (abide, remain) is frequent in Johannine vocabulary to express the permanency of relationship between Father and Son and between Son and Christian.[14] The relationship of Jesus and his disciples is patterned on that between the Father and the Son. This teaching is developed in the Last Discourse (see 14:10-11; 17:21, 23), where it is clear that the intimate indwelling of Father and Son is being transmitted through the Son to the Christian. This indwelling is sacramentalized and strengthened in the Eucharist.

The Vine and the Branches (15:1-17)

Another Gospel passage in which most commentators detect Johannine eucharistic theology is the figure of the vine and the branches (15:1-17). This passage might well be meant to serve as the cup parallel to the bread of life discourse.[15] The vine was a recognized eucharistic symbol at the time the Gospel of John reached its final form, as we know from the eucharistic prayer in the Didache: "And concerning the Eucharist, hold Eucharist thus: First concerning the Cup, 'We give thanks, our Father, for the Holy Vine of David your child, which you made known to us through Jesus your child...'" (IX:1-2). The parallel to the bread of life discourse is reinforced by the *egō eimi* statement, "I am the true vine" (15:1; see v 5), corresponding to "I am the bread of life" (6:35). The discourse takes place at the Last Supper, where the presence of the cup evokes a connection with the Eucharist.[16]

---

[14]Brown, *The Gospel I-XII,* Appendix I, 510-12.

[15]MacGregor, "The Eucharist," 112.

[16]Brown, *The Gospel XIII-XXI,* 672-74.

The vine was an established biblical symbol for Israel. Israel was a vine transplanted from Egypt (Ps 80:9), a sturdy vine which later became degenerate (Jer 2:21). The image is enlarged to that of the vineyard in the famous song of Isaiah (5:1-7). Jesus used the figure of the vineyard in the parable of the wicked husbandmen (Mk 12:1-12; Mt 21:33-46; Lk 20:9-10) and in other Synoptic parables (Mt 20:1-16; 21:28-32; Lk 13:6-9). In the Johannine passage Jesus does something new, applying the vine image to himself and his followers. The emphasis is on the relationship between Jesus and the disciples, but there may also be the subtle hint that this is the new Israel.[17]

The primary message of the vine imagery is that because Jesus is the source of life, a disciple must remain united with him to continue to live. Here we encounter again the theme of "abiding" in Jesus; the verb *menein* appears eleven times in these verses. The explanation of the vine symbolism in verses 7-17 emphasizes love: "As the Father has loved me, so have I loved you; abide in my love" (v 9). The greatest kind of love is "that a man lay down his life for his friends" (v 13). This reference to Jesus' sacrificial death is another allusion to the eucharistic theme. Those who would remain united to Jesus, so that divine life may be communicated to them as to branches of a vine, must have the same dedication to love as he, self-sacrificing love. This is very similar to the theme of the cup in Mark's Gospel (Mk 10:38-45; 14:36). Later in John's passion narrative Jesus will ask: "Shall I not drink the cup which the Father has given me?" (18:11).

Earlier we noted that John brings an emphasis on the benefit of the Eucharist for the individual believer both now and in the future. The bread of life discourse can be read in an individualistic way, without any sense of community awareness. The community dimension of the Eucharist is revealed in the imagery of the vine and the branches. Commentators have compared John's image for the relationship of Jesus and his disciples with Paul's idea of the body of Christ. The union with

---

[17] *Ibid.*, 670. This is disputed by Barnabas Linders, *The Gospel of John* (New Century Bible; Greenwood, S. C.: Attic, 1977), 487.

Jesus is still unique and personal, but it carries with it the consequence of union with others also connected to the vine, and responsibilities, especially that of self-sacrificing love.

Two more passages in John's Gospel are worthy of mention in connection with the Eucharist.[18] The first is 19:34, where the soldier opens the side of Jesus with a spear, "and at once there came out blood and water." The primary meaning here is twofold: Jesus really did die (against the Docetists), and his death releases the living water of the Spirit which has been foretold earlier in the Gospel. The eucharistic allusion arises from this Spirit theme. John the Baptist had introduced Jesus as the one who would "baptize with the Holy Spirit" (1:33), and Jesus told Nicodemus of the necessity of being born of "water and the Spirit"(3:50). At the feast of Tabernacles Jesus proclaimed, "If any one thirsts, let him come to me and drink. He who believes in me, as the scripture has said, 'Out of his heart shall flow rivers of living water.' Now this he said about the Spirit"(7:37-39). The blood seems to be a reference to the fact that the gift of the Spirit could be given only through the death of Jesus. The outpouring of the water and the blood at the moment of Jesus' death signifies the release of the Spirit, which comes to the believer through baptism. There is definitely a reference to Christian baptism here, and probably also to the Eucharist as the sacrament which sustains the Spirit life.[19]

In John 21, considered an appendix to the Gospel, the meal of bread and fish is also evocative of the Eucharist (vv 9-13). The description "Jesus . . . took the bread and gave it to them, and so with the fish" is an allusion to the scene of the multiplication of loaves (6:11), which has eucharistic implications in all the Gospel accounts. The recognition of Jesus at

---

[18]References to the Eucharist at Cana (2:1-11) or in the feet-washing at the Last Supper (13:3-20) are doubtful; but see MacGregor, "The Eucharist," 111, 113-14.

[19]Eduard Schweizer finds "unquestionably" a reference to the two sacraments as continuing signs of the reality of the Incarnation: *The Lord's Supper,* 8-9. Like Raymond Brown, *The Gospel of John XIII-XXI,* 950-51, he relates 19:34 to 1 Jn 5:6-8; "This is he who came by water and blood, Jesus Christ. . . "; see also Herbert Klos, *Die Sakramente im Johannesevangelium: Vorkommen und Bedeutung von Taufe, Eucharistie und Büsse im vierten Evangelium* (Stuttgarter Bibelstudien 46; Stuttgart: Katholisches Bibelwerk, 1970), 80-81.

this meal is similar to the experience of the disciples at Emmaus, where they knew him in the "breaking of the bread" (Lk 24:30-31). "None of the disciples dared ask him, 'Who are you?' They knew it was the Lord" (v 12). Consonant with Johannine symbolism, the breakfast here is an act of communion with the Lord who is known by faith.[20]

Summary

Though John has a profound eucharistic theology, he does not record the institution of the Eucharist at the Last Supper. Apparently he wanted to avoid isolating the Eucharist from Jesus' earthly life as an institution for the time of the Church. He shows the Eucharist flowing from Jesus' words and deeds during the ministry. This emphasis is part of John's doctrine of the Incarnation. Jesus is the word made flesh responding to humanity's deepest aspirations. He communicates eternal life to the believer through the self-gift of his whole life and his death.

The discourse on the bread of life in Chapter 6 presents the Eucharist as the sacramental climax of the Incarnation for the individual. In focusing on the meaning of the bread for each participant, John takes a different perspective from that of Paul, who emphasizes the meaning of the community action. The communitarian dimension is evoked in John's image of the vine and the branches (15:1-17).

[20]Lindars, *The Gospel of John*, 632.

Afterword

As the expression of the living faith of the followers of Jesus, the Eucharist can never be a static reality. The interplay between the gospel and the ever changing circumstances and demands of daily life focuses for the individual in personal prayer and for the community in public worship. Here the meaning of salvation in Christ is proclaimed, probed, validated.

In the biblical sources we discover a Lord's Supper that is evolving in practice as its meaning is deepening in the experience of the participants. We may be surprised to find that things we have taken for granted are not as simple as they seemed. We do not know exactly what Jesus said and did at the Last Supper, nor is there agreement in every detail on his motivation. The institution narrative has been preserved in two different traditions, Mark/Matthew and Paul/Luke. Neither of these traditions report the last meal of Jesus in a "pure" form. All have been affected by liturgical practice and other influences.

One response to discoveries like these is pessimism about discerning Jesus' meaning and purpose with regard to the Eucharist; another is indifferentism. But there is an important distinction between authentic development and careless change. The early communities did not feel the need to parrot Jesus' words or to examine the minute details of his actions in order to preserve them. They were convinced of Jesus' presence in their midst. They had interiorized his gospel as spirit and life rather than just words and actions and ideas; and they felt free to portray Jesus out of the depth of their faith experience in ways that would best communicate the reality of Jesus and his message.

They did not, however, simply draw upon their hearts for the information they passed on. They were heirs and custodians of something precious they had received, the Christian faith tradition, which had been carefully preserved and communicated by the eyewitnesses and their generation. This concern for faithful adherence to the tradition, especially by constant contact with the sources, remains a perennial commitment of the disciples of Jesus. The present study of the Eucharist in the New Testament is an effort in that direction. The living Church must constantly be corrected and adjusted to the norm established in the Christian Scriptures.

At the same time, a study like this underscores again how important Church context and experience is in shaping response to the biblical witness. We Christians read the same words about the origins and interpretations of the Lord's Supper, but they may influence our worship and our understanding quite differently. Scholars apply the same tools of exegesis, but arrive at different conclusions. As elsewhere, here we are faced again with the fact that the Bible does not interpret itself. The Church, though guided and corrected by the word, is the divinely appointed interpreter of the word. Contradictory interpretations of the biblical witness to the Eucharist, this central Christian reality, are an inevitable consequence of Church division. They will serve a redemptive purpose if they goad us on in our quest for Christian unity.

Our study reminds us, too, that we are not to look to the Bible for a model first-century Church to copy. The New Testament does not present the times nearest to Jesus as a Golden Age to which we must constantly return. We are to bring the life of Christ and the message of the gospel to new expression in our own day and in our own way, while making sure that our Christian life and eucharistic practice is an authentic development from the original expression. We do not find in the New Testament a Church beginning from some ground zero, but a Church already evolving through different styles and approaches and searching for deeper meaning.

The Last Supper of Jesus with his disciples was a surprise to them in some ways because of the particular meaning he gave to it as he shared his body and blood with them before his death. But in other ways it was a familiar setting, because the sharing of meals had had a significant role during the years of his public ministry. Jesus' open table fellowship was a prophetic sign of God's love and openness to everyone, of the availability of salvation to all. During that last meal together, the disciples learned more about Jesus and about themselves and their relationship to him, and later on when they shared the Lord's Supper, they penetrated even further into the divine mystery that had come into their midst.

Every subsequent age has continued to probe the eucharistic experience and to enrich the following generations with insight. We do not give the Eucharist a new meaning, but plumb the riches of the reality that is portrayed in the New Testament. The encounter with eucharistic patterns and themes in the biblical sources can inspire fidelity to the authentic tradition and evoke new appreciation of the Eucharist we already know from our own experience.

Suggested Reading

Raymond E. Brown, *The Churches the Apostles Left Behind* (New York: Paulist, 1984). This book is not devoted specifically to the Eucharist, but it describes the context for developments in early Church doctrine and practice.

Helmut Gese, *Essays on Biblical Theology* (Minneapolis: Augsburg, 1981). An important essay in this collection is "The Origin of the Lord's Supper."

Joachim Jeremias, *The Eucharistic Words of Jesus* (New York: Scribner's, 1966). A classic study which is still influential in any discussion of the Eucharist in the New Testament.

Robert J. Karris, *Luke: Artist and Theologian: Luke's Passion Account as Literature* (Theological Inquiries; New York: Paulist, 1985). Chapter 4, "The Theme of Food," culminates in a discussion of Luke's account of the Last Supper.

I.H. Marshall, *Last Supper and Lord's Supper* (Grand Rapids: Eerdman's, 1980). Readable analysis of the New Testament data with attention to the first-century context.

John Reumann, *The Supper of the Lord: The New Testament, Ecumenical Dialogues, and Faith and Order on Eucharist* (Philadelphia: Fortress, 1985). Report on the trends in ecumenical dialogue on the Eucharist during the last thirty years, prefaced by a review of recent biblical research.

Donald Senior, *The Passion Series* (Wilmington: Glazier). These studies of the passion accounts investigate the theology influencing each evangelist's presentation of the Last Supper. Two of the four projected volumes have appeared: (Mark (1984) and Matthew (1985).

Scripture Index

Scripture Index

OLD TESTAMENT

NEW TESTAMENT

Index

BV 823 .K63 1991

Kodell, Jerome.

The Eucharist in the Ne
Testament /